A Long Way To Nome

The Serum Run '25 Expedition

The Chronicle of a Musher, His Adopted Sled Dogs, and Their Pursuit of an Alaskan Dream

Photo credit Don Duncan

Von E. Martin

A Call of the Wild Huskies Book

A Call of the Wild Huskies Book

To order this title or receive more information, please contact:

Von Martin at NorthwestMusher@aol.com

Or visit www.CalloftheWildHuskies.com

Book cover photo credit: Amy Whisler

Reverse cover photo credit: Dr. Brian Trimble

Book design and all photos by author unless otherwise noted

ISBN 1449912613

Printed in the United States of America

First Printing December 2009

Dedicated to the memory of

Bear, Cub, Jet and the dogs
who gave their lives in service
of the original 1925 Serum Run relay

Col. Norman D. Vaughan,
whose personal vision gave birth to the
The Serum Run '25 Expedition

My Dad, Eldon Meril Martin, who lived to see
his son realize the dream of a lifetime

And for Wolfie, whose spirit helped to guide me
throughout the 2009 Serum Run '25 Expedition

Acknowledgements

To my wife Judith, for your love, support and the creation of the many home prepared "gourmet meals" that sustained me throughout the expedition. My mother Carole for skillfully sewing 1,500 dog booties, making countless equipment repairs, and believing in my dream. My granddaughter Sydney for creating the original artwork for my 2009 Serum Run "Mail Cachets".

To my stepdaughter Misty Cooney, son-in-law Mickey, and granddaughter Sydney for the gift of a top notch Cabela's Parka. Paula & Richard Pateman for the spinning & knitting the beautiful scarf and cap made from Wolfie's wool. My brother Ray for smoking trout and salmon snacks for the trail. Don Duncan for persuading me to undertake this extraordinary journey, for your friendship, encouragement, advice, and for fabricating my dog team picket lines. Margaret Black for encouraging me to make the run. Laura Daugereau for the very special huskies you have "rehomed" with my kennel throughout the years, for your friendship, professional mentoring, and for creating the beautiful fur ruff for my snowsuit. Rick & Sandy Larson for "rehoming" their superb huskies Willow, Birch, Cherry and Blackjack with our kennel.

To Dana Knight of Alaska Airlines Air Cargo for special arrangement of Teek's rush shipment from Seattle to Anchorage. Arlen Veleke of the Lacey Cabalas' store for your support. Becky & Joe Loveless of Alpine Outfitters for sewing the dog team's blankets & harnesses, providing new dog collars, making equipment loans, sled rigging, helping with dog inoculations, special pricing for Pursuit & Momentum dog kibble, the donation of 4 lbs of Impact and 50 lbs of packaged lamb trail snacks for the dog team, and especially for the priceless gift of a beautiful scarf made from Wolfie's wool. To my friends Terry & Barbara DeKruyf for the gift of 150 lbs of meat for the dogs and to Don and Chris Brosnan for the loan of their digital video camera. I am also grateful to Dan Schreiber of the Centralia Chronicle for his colorful news coverage of our expedition experience.

To Jo & Ken Walch, my very gracious Alaskan host family in Big Lake, Alaska who cheerfully cared for Sol-leks during the expedition. I am also grateful to Jo and Ken for picking up my entire dog team at the airport upon their return from the expedition. To Judy Carrick, my dog truck driver and dog handler. To Erin McLarnon, expedition musher team leader, and Kent Kantowski, expedition trail boss, for your capable and experienced leadership. To Amy Whisler, my snow machine partner and medical team specialist who expertly transported my supplies every mile of the trail. Evie Wakulenko RN, expedition medical team specialist for her care of Teek on the trail, Dr. Jerry Vanek DVM, expedition veterinarian, Dr. Lyndall Soule DVM, Dr. Val Stuve, DVM of Aurora Animal Clinic in Fairbanks, AK; Dr. Dale Marker DVM & staff at the Jackson Hwy Veterinary Clinic in Chehalis, WA. To Ilana Kingsley and Greg Newby for care offered to Blackjack while kenneled at their home near Fairbanks, AK.

I particularly wish to thank for the following people for their financial sponsorship of our 2009 Serum Run '25 Expedition huskies. Ron & Phyllis Campbell, Kathy Cooney, Kat Harder, Jackie, Malcolm, and Dianna Currie, Terry and Barbara deKruyf, Charlie & Joyce Davis, Jane Siple DeWitt, Ralph & Barbara Thomberg, Kim Blomsness, Darryl Corfman & Family, Kathleen Barriteau, and Sandy Romanek.

To each of you I offer my most sincere and heartfelt thanks. Every one of you were responsible for making our expedition experience possible. On behalf of our expedition team – Thank You.

Von E. Martin
2009 Serum Run '25 Musher

Contents

"Wolfie"
1992 - 2005
Wolfie, a female Alaskan Malamute, was the genesis
of my introduction to the world of running sled dogs

For the Love of a Dog

"If you talk to animals they will talk with you and you will know each other"

- Chief Dan George

"The Little Ewok"
Wolfie at 9 weeks of age

Of the many questions I am asked about running sled dogs, the one I most often hear is, "How did you ever get involved in dog mushing?" My answer is surprisingly simple. My tenure in the world of sled dogs all began with a dog named Wolfie. She was an Alaskan Malamute who came into my life as a young pup and forever changed my world. She was also the beginning of a long string of circumstances that would eventually lead me to the Serum Run '25 Expedition across Alaska.

January 1993

My wife Judith and I accepted a midwinter invitation for a dinner party in Bothell, Washington. As we parked our car in the long driveway of our host, my attention was drawn to a movement along the neighbor's fence line. Silently studying our arrival was the most magnificent dog I had ever seen. It was a large grey Alaskan Malamute in full winter's coat. Moments later it was joined by another equally beautiful animal - then another - and still another. Their majestic grace captured my attention and as we entered the home of our friends, I couldn't stop thinking about them.

Later that evening our dinner host's neighbor stopped by for a visit. When I remarked about her beautiful dogs, she uttered the unforgettable words that established the genesis of my dog team journey across Alaska. "We have new puppies born just last month", she announced. "Would you like to see them?"

What could it hurt to see their new puppies? We marched next door to visit their new "little bundles of joy". Entering a small den we witnessed a whelping box containing eight wiggling, fuzzy forms that cavorted and yelped. One by one, they were lifted from their pen and placed upon the floor. Almost immediately a chubby, sable colored pup waddled straight up to me and gazed into my face. Her little brown eyes shined like tiny almonds and in them I could see someone I already knew. It was my Wolfie.

A few weeks later, my wife and I returned for that wiggling, chubby "Ewok" who struggled in my arms and howled all the way home. Once there, I placed my little charge into her new kennel. Almost immediately she threw back her fuzzy head, pointed her nose to the sky, and let loose with a

"Wolfie in Her Prime"
Age 6 years

soaring wolf-like howl that amazed me with its intensity. I was sure she could be heard several blocks away. "Well," my wife exclaimed. "I hope you're happy . . . you finally got your *wolf*."

I aptly named this vocal little girl, Wolfie. Already missing her mother, brothers, and sisters, little Wolfie howled and howled in protest. Before long I was forced to bring her inside the garage where I spent a fitful night's sleep on the cold concrete floor next to her cozy bed of blankets. Although I did not know it on that first night, I had just taken the first step that, one day, would set me upon a journey to Nome, Alaska by dog team.

October 16th, 2005

The veterinarian showed me into a small exam room where Wolfie looked up to greet me with a weak smile. Then we were left alone. Kneeling before her, I took her huge bear-like head in my hands and with the greatest courage I could muster, spoke to her in soft words. "Wolfie" I said, "I have saved a special gift to you as my very last". Looking directly into her eyes I added, "This will be my *greatest* gift of love". I was about to help Wolfie out of the pain and suffering from a terrible disease that now swept through her nearly thirteen year old body. With a steady hand I signed the authorization to put her down and cremate her remains. Then I returned my arms around her luxurious sable coat that I had come to love so well.

"Constant Companions"
Throughout her lifetime, Wolfie and I traveled hundreds of miles together on countless wilderness adventures
The Umatilla National Forest, Oregon 1998

Minutes earlier I had stood by as my veterinarian pointed out the grim details of Wolfie's X-rays. What they revealed was the worst possible news. Cancer. "I'm so sorry," my vet looked at me as he spoke in a low, even tone. Tragically, the fatal disease had swept through much of Wolfie's poor body. I knew what was coming next. I had been mentally preparing myself for this day and I had lovingly planned for every detail.

For nearly 13 years, Wolfie had been my constant companion. In her lifetime she had logged hundreds of miles in harness and had taken us to two 1st Place NWSDA Ski-jor Championships as we raced throughout Washington, Oregon, and Idaho. During those years, Wolfie guided me deep into the wonderful world of running sled dogs. She made many classroom visits and twice participated in dog shows at the Western Washington State Fair. Throughout Wolfie's lifetime she taught me all she knew.

Once, in spite of her fear of water, Wolfie tried to pull me ashore while I swam in a river because, somehow, she thought I was in danger. Together we had traveled over 250,000 miles in my pickup truck. Each ride always began with her soaring wolf-like howl. In her senior years, Wolfie helped to haul timber from the woods behind our cabin, and she became particularly fond of camping in our tipi on balmy summer nights. In her final years, Wolfie relished her new role as "mascot" to our kennel of adopted sled dogs as we added Alaskan and Siberian Huskies in growing numbers. She especially enjoyed her daily free runs throughout the ranch property, and most particularly, our quiet morning walks together.

"A Strong and Steady Puller"
Wolfie took great pleasure in her ski-jor races as seen here on Mt Hood, OR

With the greatest possible care, my vet prepared Wolfie's lethal injection while I held her in my arms and showered her with carefully practiced words of love and praise. I left nothing out. And in those final minutes I issued her a solemn pledge. "Wolfie", I announced, "if I ever go to Nome by dog team, I promise to take you along to help show me the way". Then as the lethal fluid was released into her veins, I held her warm, wooly face against mine and told her over and over, "I love you". So strong was her hold on life that even in those final moments she heroically struggled against death. Then as she finally began to slip away I softly whispered in her ear, "I release you. Now go wait for me on the other side. Wait for me. Now fly girl . . . *fly*." Wolfie exhaled long and completely with a guttural groan that weakened before rising into a faint whine. I drew her final parting breath deep into my lungs and held it there for a time. Then she was gone.

"Wolfie's Last Night at Home"
Wolfie sleeps quietly on her favorite blanket in the log cabin
Age 12 years 10 months

After a few moments I rose to my feet and marveled over her perfect form lying so peacefully. She looked so completely beautiful, even with the life gone out of her. Through streaming tears, I took a clipping from her wooly coat and cut the collar from around her neck - a symbolic gesture of her release from service. As I held that collar in my hands, I pondered over my final promise to her. Would a journey to Nome with Wolfie ever really be possible?

Perhaps someday, if I could just find a way, I would drive my own dog team across Alaska to Nome. And in the sled would be Wolfie's little tin of ashes. Only then would my promise be fulfilled. And in return, Wolfie's spirit would join me to cheerfully show the way.

"Oh Summer Days"
Cheerful little Cherry (foreground) and some of Von Martin's huskies enjoy
the dog yard's shady cool lawn on a warm summer day at his log cabin home
June 30th, 2008

The Decision to Go

"Dream Big and Dare to Fail"

- Col. Norman D. Vaughan

February 2006

Our New "Fuzzie" Girl
Our new little Malamute pup bears an
uncanny resemblance to her namesake

After the death of Wolfie, I returned to the business of upgrading our kennel, the addition of new sled dogs, and running races in the lower forty eight. For nearly three years the notion of a trip to Nome by dog team was returned to the background of my unanswered dreams. That winter, my wife Judith and I loaded our entire kennel of thirteen huskies into the dog truck and drove a thousand miles to Wyoming for the Casper Mountain Sled Dog Race. It was a torturous mid-winter race and it was my first introduction to truly cold temperatures.

The trail took my team of eight huskies over the top of treeless Casper Mountain, ten thousand feet in elevation where blizzard-like winds plunged the wind chill factor to forty-seven degrees below zero. There I was introduced to the disorienting effects of hypothermia. Late in the race, I encountered what my befuddled mind read as a confusing trail marker to turn left *or* right. Holding my team at the intersection, I studied the marker through frosted goggles in total disbelief. How could this possibly be? Finally, after a long hesitation, I directed my team onto the right hand trail and away we went - in the wrong direction.

After a frigid detour that added many miles to our run, we finally found our way back. Although my team of huskies held up well in those sub-zero temperatures, I was directed to a warming tent for a brief period of observation and recovery. I had fallen victim to the mind bending effects of dehydration. It was a lesson hard learned. And it was a lesson that, one day, would serve me well in Alaska.

Shortly after the Casper Mountain Race, I made a new addition to our kennel. She was a sable colored Alaskan Malamute pup and my first since raising Wolfie, as all of our huskies were adopted as adults. The new puppy, conceived at the time of Wolfie's death, bore an almost uncanny resemblance to her. I named the woolly pup "Fuzzie", a favorite nickname of her bygone predecessor. Throughout that winter, Fuzzie's comical puppy antics help to ease the loss of my old friend but did not diminish her memory or my unfulfilled promise that, one day, we would cross Alaska together by dog team.

September 2007

Late in the summer of 2007, Blackjack, a gentle natured, four year old Alaskan Husky with a wide happy smile joined our kennel. Born and raised in the kennel of Iditarod musher Dee Dee Jonrowe, he had found himself, due to circumstances, shuffled from kennel to kennel in search of the right home. Then I received a call from Laura Daugereau, a good friend and mushing colleague, who thought Blackjack might make the perfect addition for our mountainous back country mushing adventures.

"Always Smiling"
Blackjack displays his typically happy smile following a "de-skunking" bath

Powerful and sturdy but too slow to make a first string Iditarod dog team, Blackjack was in need of a new home. By mutual arrangement with his current owners, Rick and Sandy Larson, Blackjack was driven from his home in Montana to Spokane, Washington where I met him for the first time.

He was a real throwback to the working Alaskan village dogs of yesteryear. Full coated and medium boned, Blackjack, aka "Jack", would make the perfect addition to our growing kennel. Unfortunately, he had an experience involving a skunk shortly before leaving Montana. This made for a *very* fragrant drive back to our ranch in my little Jeep Wrangler on a sweltering summer day. However the "fumes" never bothered Blackjack. He just smiled at the passing scenery and wagged his tail throughout the long six hour drive home.

In the winter following his placement with our kennel, Blackjack proved his value in harness during several races, including the Cascade Quest Sled Dog Race in the steep Washington Cascades. While he did not posses the fluid lope of our swiftest Alaskan Huskies, he was well matched to the sturdy power and endurance of our heavier Siberians. During that winter, my mind formed a dim thought that perhaps my dogs might be better suited for longer, steady marches across difficult terrain, rather than the shorter mid-distance races we typically ran.

While conducting research on the history of sled dogs recruited for the early Antarctic expeditions, my mind had become captivated by the uncanny ability of those dogs to haul heavy loads over great distances. The idea of experiencing an expedition by dog team, rather than competitive racing, tempted my imagination. Then spring arrived, the wintery trails melted away, and so did my musings of a long distance experience.

May 2008

That spring I made plans to rebuild and upgrade our kennel facility. On a glorious sunny day in May the phone rang at my log cabin home. "Hey Von, this is Laura Daugereau", came the familiar voice. Just weeks earlier, Laura had become the first woman from the state of Washington to complete the Alaska Iditarod Sled Dog Race. Today she was calling to interest me in an offer to "rehome" three of her Iditarod finishers with my kennel. The siblings, Birch, Willow, and Cherry, were Alaskan Huskies who, during their lifetimes, had completed more than forty races including two Iditarod races.

Raised by Rick Larson in Montana, the three eight year olds were now being retired from Iditarod racing. Healthy, strong, and particularly well socialized, all three were still capable of

"All Business"
Characterized by a reserved and "aim to please" personality, Willow maintains watch over his siblings in the dog yard

multiple long runs. During a discussion regarding their future, Rick and Laura agreed that Birch, Willow, and Cherry might be well suited for an extended mushing career with our smaller kennel. I cheerfully agreed.

In June, Laura delivered the three new additions from Montana and even pitched in to help complete their new kennels. Suddenly our little kennel had swollen to seventeen huskies, and of these only three were retired.

Early the next morning, while the sun still hung low behind the tree line, I moved my huskies from their kennels into the dog yard where they enjoyed a romp in the cool grass. As I sipped a cup of coffee and watched the dogs at play, I began to ponder their true potential. Combined as a large team, exactly what were these dogs *really* capable of?

July 2008

In early July I happened across the website of Don Duncan, my longtime friend and fellow musher. There he had posted his bid to return to Alaska in 2009 for a second Serum Run '25 expedition. His statement, superimposed over a stirring photo of

"Big Baby Blues"
Birch's freckled muzzle and heavy dark brows perched above big blue eyes offer him the look of a Disney-like character

his dog team running on the Yukon River in 2007, included a rousing poem by Robert Service entitled "Spirit of the Yukon" which begins;

"The Wease"
Cherry, aka "The Wease", petite little sister to Birch and Willow, is nicknamed for her soft Weasel-like coat and playfully "slippery" antics

"The strong life that knows no harness,
the wilds where the caribou call,
the freshness, the freedom, the farness,
Oh God! How I'm stuck on it all."

After reading those words, my mind turned to the prospect of running in this event. I was already familiar with the Serum Run '25 expedition and had even spent an afternoon with it's founder, Col. Norman Vaughan at his Anchorage home in 2005. Some years earlier, he had created the semi-annual expedition to honor the original mushers and their heroic dogs who carried life saving Diphtheria anti-toxin from Nenana, deep in the Alaskan interior, approximately 800 miles to Nome on the Bering Sea coast.

Sometimes confused with the Iditarod, a marathon sled dog race from Anchorage to Nome, the Serum Run '25 expedition was conceived as a long distance, mid-winter journey to retrace the original 1925 route across Alaska. Along the 800 mile route stops are made at each village to deliver health education programs and remember the original mushers and their teams. Comprised of about ten dog teams, the Serum Run '25 is supported by snow machines

"Jam For a Living Legend"

The late Col. Norman Vaughan, founder of the Serum Run '25 expedition, cheerfully accepts a jar of homemade jam during Von Martin and wife Judith's visit to his Anchorage home in October 2005. Col. Vaughan, principle dog driver for Byrd's 1928 Antarctic Expedition, passed away at age 100 years.

Even so, a major concern was the age of my dogs. Nearly all had been racing for many years and most no longer possessed the speed of younger dogs who dominated local races. My best leader, Chewbacca, would turn eleven in the coming winter. Six more would celebrate their ninth birthdays. Two would be eight years old and my youngest would be going on five. In another two years, most of my dogs would approach retirement. There could be little doubt - if I had any ideas about running my dogs in the Serum Run '25 expedition, it would have to be in the coming winter. It was a journey these dogs deserved and given their ages, one they were probably best suited for. It was also, I believed, an adventure they would particularly enjoy.

July 7, 2008 - (e-mail to Don Duncan)

"If there was just one event I ran next season, it would be the Serum Run. I've got 12 dogs that I'm confident could make the run. Among them are 3 Gee-Haw leaders and 2 trail leaders. But the logistics of my job would never allow for it - and then there is the money . . . a lot of money. But I don't need to tell you about all that - and the whole logistics thing!"

hauling expedition supplies, and most importantly, food for the dogs.

For more than ten years, my dogs and I had traveled throughout the Pacific Northwest to race in weekend mushing events. The winning teams of these races, the longest of which totaled just seventy-five miles, were often dominated by swift, delicately coated husky-pointer crosses.

By comparison to the fastest dogs at local races, my eclectic collection of Siberian and Alaskan huskies were typically heavier coated and well muscled from back country training in the steep Washington Cascades. With the addition of my new Iditarod finishers, Birch, Willow, and Cherry, I began to consider they might be better suited for multiple hour runs at the steady trot demanded by endurance runs. For the first time, I studied my dogs in the yard with an eye for the Serum Run '25 expedition.

"Silver Faced Gentleman"

Chewbacca, Von's principle lead dog, was already a silver faced senior by the summer of 2008. "Chewy" would celebrate his eleventh birthday during the 2009 Serum Run '25 expedition.

14

July 16, 2008 - (e-mail reply from Don Duncan**)**

"I think we are at similar points in life. We have dogs that are at the age to be able to do something big, we are at the age where we can still do something big, and the economy is teetering on the edge of an unknown that may soon make it financially impossible to do something big. I realize work, money, and life in general are huge obstacles, but if you want to have the most spiritual and fulfilling odyssey in this life with your dogs, I would encourage you to figure out a way to do the Serum Run. Please think hard about this . . ."

Encouraged by my friend's words, I began to give serious consideration to taking my dogs up to Alaska. With the recent addition of our new huskies, the way the dogs looked in the yard, and the good health I was still enjoying, providence seemed to be showing the way. Almost before I knew it, plans to go to Alaska were propelling us like a run-away freight train.

On a hot July day in 2008, I climbed the stairs to my wife's home office. Clutched in my hands was the Serum Run '25 expedition application and instruction documents. Neatly placing the one inch thick stack of papers upon her desk, I turned to Judy and calmly announced, "As of this moment I have absolutely no idea how this would be possible, but this is something I really want to do."

Judy looked at me and was quiet for a minute before turning her attention to the neatly stacked application on her desk. I had already thought about the many objections she *could* have offered at that moment. But I was both surprised and encouraged by her answer. Picking up the Serum Run expedition application in both hands, she studied it for a time and simply asked, "So how much is all this going to cost?"

"King of the Pack"

Zyphr, once the finest sled dog in Von's kennel, reflects upon his bygone glory days. Sadly, this thirteen year old "King of the Pack" was too elderly to be considered for the Serum Run expedition and was retired from service in 2008.

My wife's question was well founded. By my best estimates, out of pocket expenses could exceed $10,000. Not only would joining the Serum Run expedition present a financial strain but there would be lost wages due to time away from work. Would my employer be willing to grant a two month sabbatical? How would we manage the care of our dogs left behind? Could I schedule the time to properly train our huskies for nearly 1,000 miles? Above all, would our team be chosen by the Serum Run selection committee? These questions were just the tip of the iceberg. Potential road blocks would rise up to challenge our "dream" every step of the way.

"All the Better to See You With"
Alternate team dog, Teek, a Siberian Husky with distinctive blue and brown eyes, rests in harness following his first Alaskan training run. Teek was rushed by air freight to replace Sol-leks shortly before the expedition
February 18, 2009

The Expedition Huskies

"It's all about the dogs . . . "

- author unknown

"CHEWBACCA"
Alaskan Husky - Command Leader

Chewbacca - aka "Chewy", senior member and principal lead dog for Von's expedition team is a near look alike of *Balto*, hero of the original 1925 Serum Run. Chewy would celebrate his eleventh birthday during the 2009 Serum Run expedition. Unfettered by the worst of weather conditions including white-outs, headwinds, and minus zero degree temperatures, the calm and capable leadership possessed by this amazing husky are conveyed in the riveting gaze of his strong, steady eyes. Gentle and reserved by nature, this "silver tipped gentleman" can be counted on for an honest day's work each and every mile.

As the training coach to my dog team, one of my goals is to help keep the "joy" in every run. Whenever I see the dogs cavort and yelp during harnessing and hookup I am reminded that these dogs only run because they *want* to run. And it is that "want" that I make every effort to cultivate from the first mile of training through the end of the season.

During dry land training, water and bowls are carried to properly maintain hydration on even the shortest runs. Sturdy cordura booties are fitted on the dogs as needed. I am quick to offer praise for good performance and encouragement when the going gets tough. During each run I am on the lookout for strengths and weaknesses, both physical and mental, that are revealed by each dog. Above all, I work to maintain a relationship of trust with each dog that must never be betrayed.

Trust the dogs. It is a saying as old as mushing. But while it is common knowledge among seasoned dog drivers, it was another early lesson I came by in a difficult way. Wolfie, my first sled dog, was an outstanding gee-haw leader, that is she was responsive to verbal commands to turn right or left. Although Wolfie did not run with the team, she was still an exceptional lead dog who taught me my first lesson about trusting your dog's instincts on the trail.

It happened many years ago during one of our ski-jor races, a competitive event paring one or two harnessed dogs connected to a skier. The race which is held on a heavily wooded trail system near Mount Hood, Oregon. is shared by numerous sled dog classes. The length of the trail includes several cutoffs and intersections that have to be successfully negotiated.

At one particular intersection, Wolfie pulled to the left. Yet I was sure we were to bear right and

"GRITS"

Alaskan Husky - Command Leader

Nephew to Chewbacca, snowy white Grits resembles a beautiful arctic wolf with his luxurious winter coat and curious amber eyes. The most responsive command leader on Von's team, Grits was a late bloomer who emerged unexpectedly as an exceptional lead dog at age eight. Confident and vocal, Grits is the playful friend of every human and every dog. Grits ran in the lead position for the entire 2009 Serum Run Expedition!

called her over. She resisted, and with a little leap and shake of her head, made her best effort to bear me over in the other direction. Grabbing the tugline with both hands, I forced her back onto the trail bearing right. With a shrug of her coat, Wolfie gave in and with a long look over her shoulder, trotted off in the direction I commanded.

Soon the spring fell out of her step. Along the way she continued to throw me occasional backward glances that seemed to check my decision. Finally, after several miles I began to realize that we, or rather that I, had lost the trail. There was nothing to do but to turn around and go back. However, the delay and extra miles run had forced us hopelessly out of the competition. Not only did we arrive at the finish dead last, we were beaten by a skier racing a Beagle.

Back at the dog truck, Wolfie sat with her back to me. Even when I called her name, she acted as if I wasn't there and refused to look at me. "Hummf", her body language seem to say, "beaten by a Beagle". Worse, by not allowing her to follow her faultless instincts on the trail, I had jeopardized her trust in me. I had paid a high price for a hard lesson learned. Trust the dogs. On very long runs this would be especially so, perhaps even life-saving, when crossing the Alaskan frontier.

There is a strong case to be made for rescued dogs. Sol-leks, a male Siberian Husky, was but one of several huskies rescued by our kennel from the animal shelter just hours before they were to be euthanized as unwanted pets. On my first meeting with Sol-leks, his tongue hung in a deep pant from his leaping, frenzied appeal to gain attention from passersby at the county shelter. Sadly, his persistent plea went ignored by all. "That dog is just too hyper", I heard someone say. Still, there was a gentleness in his eyes that seemed to belie an inner knowledge that his situation was grave. While others passed him over, I studied him long and carefully. This young Siberian Husky had all the makings of a fine sled dog.

He was wolf gray in color with a narrow, shark-faced muzzle. His snowy-white face was punctuated by deep brown eyes set narrowly below sharp prick ears and finished off with a small shiny nose, black as a lump of coal. He was slight for a Siberian husky and I estimated his weight at about forty-five pounds. Most remarkable, were his large, tight, snowshoe paws that terminated at the end of well-

"BACON"
Alaskan Husky - Command Leader
Brother to Grits, eight year old Bacon is a little shy
but when running at the front of the team, is a true
and reliable leader. Distinguished by his pink
"snow nose", Bacon is especially fond of his brother
Grits, who he always greets with a leap of joy and
a gentle paw placed upon his brother's shoulder.
A proven leader with numerous mid-distance race
finishes, Bacon poured his heart into every mile
of the journey and seemed to particularly enjoy the
expedition no matter how bad the weather got!

"WILLOW"
Alaska Husky - Trail Leader
Brother to Birch and Cherry, this Iditarod Race veteran
can be characterized by his serious, "get the job done"
personality. Reserved but powerful, Willow is an
Alaskan Husky raised by musher Rick Larson of
Montana who generously "rehomed" him together with
his brother and sister so they could enjoy their senior
years together in Von's kennel. It is heart-warming to
see these three siblings still together after such long,
distinguished racing careers. After two Iditarod race
finishes, Willow still enjoyed returning to Alaska and
helped lead the team on the mighty Yukon River.

muscled legs. Ironically, it was these powerful legs that had caused him to be placed into his perilous situation. The same capable legs that would one day serve him well throughout our many sled dog races had once carried him over countless miles of city streets and sidewalks. In his earlier life, Sol-leks had been a chronic "runaway." Guided by his own powerful instincts to run and cover great distances, he could not, or would not, be contained by his former owner. After expressing an interest in him, the shelter attendant led me into a small office where a final call was placed to his former owner. There I overheard stories of his many escapes and runaways from a home where he was no longer

"SOL-LEKS"
Siberian Husky - Trail Leader

Sol-leks, aka "Daddy's Boy", celebrated his ninth birthday during the Serum Run expedition. Sol-leks is one of Von's special huskies rescued from the county animal shelter as an unwanted pet in January of 2002. Since his adoption, Sol-leks has cheerfully run thousands of miles in harness and completed countless races. Equipped with indestructible feet and a tireless gait, Sol-leks has always been one of the hardest working dogs in Von's kennel. Sadly, Sol-leks sustained a sports injury to his left knee shortly before the expedition and was forced to be withdrawn from the team. Sol-leks now enjoys the benefits of an early retirement and a life of leisure.

wanted. After his most recent roundup, he was impounded by the county animal shelter where he now awaited a fearful fate. As his allotted "adoption" time was nearly exhausted, the restless yearling would face euthanasia by lethal injection early the next day.

Following the call, the shelter attendant returned me to his kennel where he continued a desperate appeal to anyone who might take notice. When I asked for a visit, the steel gate to his kennel was sprung open and the desperate dog flew swiftly into my arms. To the attendants utter amazement, the wolf gray husky lay quietly cradled in my arms and licked my chin. "Write up his adoption," I told the attendant. "I'm taking this boy home."

In the years that followed, Sol-leks covered thousands of miles on the trail with our team of adopted huskies and completed dozens of sled dog races. Often he would lead our team on these long runs and in return, sought only his daily feeding, a kind word, and most particularly, my company. Eventually, his thankful devotion and gentle ways earned him the nickname "Daddy's Boy", an endearment that fits him perfectly.

Teek, a luxuriously coated Siberian Husky whose raccoon-colorings are tipped with glimmering threads of silver, is another of our animal shelter rescues. At our first meeting he was but half grown and laying with his back to the kennel gate at the county shelter. While I couldn't see his face, I guessed his age at about six months. Kneeling down I called to him. Lifting his face to greet mine I almost gasped and then began to chuckle. With reserved enthusiasm, he studied me directly with his remarkable eyes. One was brown, soft, quiet, and warm. The other was icy blue, riveting, and piercing. Beginning at his freckled muzzle a wide panting smile beamed across his cheerful face. What a little beauty he was.

I knew in my heart that this husky pup probably shared a common and sad story. In all likelihood, he had been purchased as an eight-week old puppy that by six months grew into a nuisance and a trip to the county shelter. Next, a failed adoption had nearly sealed his fate. Guilty of chewing carpet and underwear, he had been returned as a reject to the county shelter. Now the six month old pup's allotted time to be adopted would expire in only hours. Without delay, I arranged for his adoption and named

"CHERRY"
Alaskan Husky - Swing Dog
This amazingly fast and petite little Alaskan Husky
has already completed two Iditarod Sled Dog Races,
the last one for musher, Laura Daugereau in 2008.
Next, this darling little girl reprised her trans-Alaska
legacy with one final encore - the 2009 Serum Run '25
expedition! Throughout the journey, Cherry helped
Tigger set the pace running as "swing dog" right
behind the leaders. All this affectionate girl wants to
do is run. Stop the team for a short break and she is
screaming and leaping in her harness to get going again!

"TIGGER"
Alaskan Husky - Swing Dog
Sister to Bacon & Grits, this darling little forty-three
pound, nine year old Alaskan Husky is the fastest dog
on the team! Able to maintain a blistering trot as fast as
the boys can run, Tigger is happiest in "swing" position
where her main job is to set the pace for the entire team.
This made her one of the hardest working dogs on the
team! Shy but very vocal, Tigger demonstrated the best
year of her career and did an outstanding job setting the
pace for every mile of the expedition. Besides a good hot
meal, Tigger eagerly awaited a nice belly rub at the end
of each day! Good things do come in "little packages".

the silver coated beauty Teek, after one of the huskies who, like Sol-leks, and Pike, were popular dog
characters from Jack London's "The Call of the Wild."

As a youth, Teek was my "happy-go-lucky" boy, a richly spirited husky, who was easily distracted
by every subtle detail of his environment. Although the other huskies ran in harness with heads bent,
tails down, while singularly focused upon the trail ahead, young Teek would stride along merrily ab-
sorbed in the minutia of every detail surrounding him - the birds soaring overhead, the movements of
the clouds, and even the rustle of leaves through the trees.

"BLACKJACK"
Alaskan Husky - Team Dog
Blackjack - aka "Jack", a 4 year old Alaskan Husky,
is the youngest dog on the team. Jack was born and
raised in Dee Dee Jonrowe's kennel in Willow, Alaska
where he ran for her team as a youngster. This forever
cheerful, hard working boy came to Von's kennel by
way of Iditarod musher Rick Larson from Montana.
Jack is a real throw back to those wonderful old style
"Alaskan Village Dogs" of yesteryear - sturdy, well
coated, and just plain hard working! He is a pleasure
to run in harness and just loves to give
great big bear hugs!

"BIRCH"
Alaskan Husky - Team Dog
Sporting a gorgeous, wavy "collie-like" coat and
the bluest eyes you ever saw, this eight year old,
two time Iditarod finisher is the bouncy, playful
brother to little Cherry. With his freckled muzzle
and heavily arched brows perched above piercing
blue eyes, Birch has both the appearance and
personality of an animated Disney-like character.
This hard working boy is amazing to watch in
harness and playful when the day's work is done!
Birch shares the namesake and resemblance to one
of the dogs with Norman Vaughan and Paul Siple
during Richard Byrd's 1928 Antarctic Expedition.

But from this free wheeling, unbridled youth slowly emerged a capable working adult who fuels the
team with his cheerful, animated antics. Although stocky and occasionally lacking the endurance of the
other dogs, Teek's delightfully cheerful attitude, good appetite, and love for the trail, secured him the
position as "alternate" for the expedition team.

Of all the dogs selected for our Serum Run '25 expedition team, none deserved a spot more than a
large, unnamed Siberian Husky we came to calling Pike. Found riddled with worms and wandering the

streets, Pike displayed a matted coat shedding in large blotchy patches at the time of his capture by county authorities.

Due to his friendly nature, Pike was kenneled at the crowded county shelter with larger, sometimes aggressive animals because of his ability to get along with any dog. Long after his adoption was I taught the true reason for his behavior. Pike is a true alpha male. Almost from the time he came to live with me, Pike effectively maintained rank and file in our growing kennel even among our largest huskies. With a special talent for maintaining order in the kennel by way of his persuasive swagger, Pike eventually ascended to the rank of "Kennel Boss".

In all the years I have run him, he has never been involved in an alteration, except one winter, years ago, when an older male challenged his even-tempered leadership. It all happened on a twenty mile training run just outside the border of Mt. Rainier National Park.

For the return leg to the truck, I placed Pike in lead with my senior command leader, a slender white Alaskan Husky named Lars, who often ran up front during training runs. During a stop along the trail to adjust the dog's tuglines and inspect their booties, Lars, who sometimes preferred running in single lead, issued a challenge to Pike. In the seconds it took for me to rush to the front of the team, Pike had already taken control of the situation by penning Lars gently but firmly onto his back. Across his face he wore a triumphant look that seemed to say, "OK boss, I've taken control of the situation. Now you can take it from here." Fortunately, there was no real harm done to either dog as is the way with true alpha dogs.

The uncanny ability to maintain order, to quell an alteration, and all without bloodshed is the true measure of an alpha dog. Many dogs are called alpha dogs. But Pike, who can effectively police the entire kennel without forced use of physical aggression, is the true measure of an alpha dog.

"PIKE"
Siberian Husky - Team Dog

If ever there was a dog who deserved a place on the 2009 Serum Run, it was this handsome "gentleman". Rescued from a county animal shelter, Pike's early life is shrouded in mystery. Found ragged and wandering on city streets, Pike faced an uncertain future before his rescue in January of 2002. Placed into harness, this large and powerful Siberian Husky consistently performs as "solid as a rock". A regal dog with soulful eyes, Pike ascended to the rank of "Kennel Boss". With a special talent for maintaining order in the kennel by way of his even temper and persuasive "swagger", Pike is truly a husky with "the heart of a lion". Of all the dogs on the team, Pike was most grateful to be included on the expedition and cheerfully ran every mile with a tight tugline!

Like the links of a chain, every dog in the team provides its own special function. Still, there is something that goes to the work of a lead dog that is special. While every husky has its unique qualities, it would be difficult, perhaps even impossible to drive a dog team over great distances without capable leaders. The mystery as to why few dogs evolve as leaders is difficult to explain and no one can be absolutely sure which dog may surprisingly reveal itself as a leader - even late in their careers. The business of what defines a great lead dog I leave to others. Legendary Iditarod mushers Susan Butcher, Lance Mackey, Martin Buser, and others have all mused at great lengths on this subject. But the deepest lessons taught to me were not in books or even at mushing seminars. They came by way of dogs in my own kennel.

Grits, a snowy white Alaskan husky with steady amber eyes, is the lead dog I almost never knew. His story is a strong case for showing how wrong I could be about one of my own dogs. And it goes to how some lead dogs evolve much later than others, and in surprising ways.

Unlike his brother Bacon, a husky who had run lead for me for several years, Grits was only content running near the middle of the team. On long runs he never seemed to settle into a proper gait and I even suspected he may have been injured before he came to live with me. On downhill lopes his legs flailed awkwardly and he had a particular dislike for snow and ice being kicked into his face by the dogs ahead of him. Even after running him for several years, I couldn't seem to find the right spot for him in the team. Were it not for the inseparable friendship he shared with his brother, I might have considered a new home for him.

Then just days before Grit's eighth birthday, I found myself in need of a co-leader for a late fall training run in the Washington Cascades. I probably chose him based upon my need for a dog who would run up front with Chewbacca without getting into trouble. In spite of his short comings as a sled dog,

"PATRICK"
Alaskan Husky - Wheel Dog
Brother to Boomer, "Patrick Henry" was born on the Fourth of July 2000 and raised by Iditarod musher Laura Daugereau. Sometimes misjudged as a wolf hybrid, this all white Alaskan Husky with golden eyes is characterized by a shy wolf-like personality. In harness, he can out perform every dog on the team. Even after nonstop sixty mile runs, Patrick acts like he has only run sixty feet while screaming to get moving again! With a perfectly matched gait to his brother Boomer, these two big boys are the "Turbo Diesel" power units of the team.

Grits is my Pollyanna. He is friend to every human and every dog and in all the years I have run him, he has never been involved in a scrap with the other huskies. What I didn't expect was a strong performance as a leader.

Perhaps it was because I occasionally ran him for short distances in lead with his brother Bacon that he had quietly picked up the vocal commands for turning left and right. As he approached his eighth

"BOOMER"
Alaskan Husky - Wheel Dog

Restless, tireless, and powerful. These are three good words to describe this eight year old Alaskan Husky with handsome brown eyes. Yet behind his serious expression lurks a silly, goofy personality that is delightfully entertaining. Always on the move, even in his kennel, Boomer is one of the first to greet you with a cheerful "Woooo - woo" and wagging tail.

One of the largest and most powerful dogs on the team, Boomer runs in the demanding wheel position, closest to the sled. At the end of each day's run, he is the first to flop on his back for a nice long belly rub!

birthday, I also noticed that his gait had evened out and now bore little resemblance to the awkward ways of his youth. At the end of his run with Chewbacca I noted in our training log, "ran very well with Chewy, very fast, strong run". Days later I recorded, "ran lead with Zyphr today - strong and steady".

Then in December of 2007 Grits led a training run in single lead, the greatest test for a lead dog, during a severe winter storm. Suddenly, almost magically, a new leader was emerging from our kennel, and he was eight years old.

Throughout the winter season I experimented by pairing him with each of our lead dogs including Zyphr, an Alaskan Husky nearing retirement, who was the finest dog in the kennel. I ran him with Chewbacca, Bacon, and even his sister Tigger. On each of these runs I tested his leadership skills by calling turns at unfamiliar intersections on the trail. Grits responded immediately, snapping into the turns without the slightest hesitation. Again and again I tested his new found skill and not once did he fail me.

During head on passes with other dog teams on narrow trails, he threaded a course straight ahead, staying to the right and always ignoring the passing dogs. We passed snowshoers and even skiers with loose dogs on the trail and it was always the same with Grits. He would guide the team, even a team of twelve dogs, safely around every obstacle. He never looked back, never seem to tire of the responsibility of picking out the best section of trail. Even on monotonous training runs over the same trail sections, never lost his enthusiasm for staying out front.

By the following spring, Grits seemed to have cheerfully settled into his new role as Command Leader and after a run on March 30th, 2008, I reserved a single high praise next to his name in the training log. "*Awesome Gee/Haw leader*".

Chewbacca, a large black Alaskan Husky with a snowy white bib, was already a veteran leader when he came to live with me. Nephew to Zyphr, my finest lead dog now retired, he had not only run as lead dog for numerous races but had even trained pups for Iditarod teams. Working together under heavy loads, Chewbacca and Zyphr would always move the team forward with their backs bent sharply above their shoulders. This forced their muzzles downward so that their noses skidded along just an

"TEEK"

Siberian Husky - Team Dog Alternate

It's Teek to the rescue! By special arrangement with Alaska Airlines Air Cargo, this hard working, "happy-go-lucky" boy arrived in Alaska only three days before the start of the expedition to replace Sol-leks. Teek is one of Von's special Siberian Huskies rescued from the county animal shelter in 1992. Imagine Teek's surprise when he was greeted by all of Von's huskies following his arrival in Alaska! Teek thoroughly enjoyed his expedition experience and was never troubled by the weather - no matter how severe things got. During the last day of the expedition, Teek never stopped working throughout an eleven hour non-stop run even as temperatures plunged to thirty-eight degrees below zero!

inch or so above the trail. No winter's storm seemed too much for them, no work too difficult for them, and never in the years I ran them together did they balk or quit on the trail.

Once, on a particularly long run during a terrible snowstorm, their endurance spared me from a bitter night stalled on a lonely trail in the Washington Cascades. More importantly, I learned how the untested capability of these dogs may be much greater than you think. It happened on a routine forty mile training run in the Gifford Pinchot National Forest between two popular winter recreation areas. We would "hook up" and depart from our camp at Johnson Creek and run to the top of a mountain pass at about 4,000 feet in elevation. Dropping down the other side, the trail crossed several streams and even a narrow icy bridge over a swift raging river. Upon our departure from Johnson Creek, we were under a light snowfall. But by the time we arrived at our turn around point near Orr Creek, a heavy winter storm had descended upon us.

Worse, the Orr Creek campground, typically full of weekend snowmobilers, was already abandoned. Not a single snow machine remained to knock down the trail and the snowfall was accumulating fast. We were still twenty miles from our dog truck and at least thirty miles from the nearest town. We were alone on the mountain.

In the next hour, the last of twilight gave way to darkness but my team leaders, Chewbacca and Zyphr, pressed on. Breaking trail on the return climb up the mountain was hard work for the dogs, and one by one several of them tired. First Teek, my heavy coated Siberian Husky floundered in the deep snow and needed a ride on the sled. Then little Tigger, demoralized by the discouraging run through ever deeper snow, begged for a ride.

I couldn't carry every dog that would tire on the return trip, so removing a dog or two at a time from the line, I offered them a ride in the sled until they recovered. It made for slow going. Worse, the batteries in my headlamp began to fail. Soon the last glimmer of light from my lamp grew dim and faded away completely. In another mile I stopped the team. The storm was blowing sideways snow, I had two dogs in the sled, we were in the pitch dark, and before us stretched a long lonely climb back over the mountain.

"Daddy's Boy"
Von Martin cradles Sol-leks, one of his Siberian Huskies, immediately following the finish of his 2008 Cascade Quest Sled Dog Race

Anchoring both snow hooks to hold the sled fast, I stomped through deep snow to the front of the team. Kneeling before Chewbacca and Zyphr, I gathered their heads in my arms and spoke to them over the wind. "Boys," I told them, "we're in a bit of trouble here. If you are too tired to go on, we'll do the best we can here for the night. But if you think we can make it back, then I'll leave it up to you." I stood up and looked down over them. Neither of these dogs had ever given up on the trail but this was different. What would they do? What had been a well-defined trail just hours earlier was now drifted over in a deep blanket of fresh snow.

Zyphr lunged in his harness and issued his squeak of a bark which always amused me because he is a large dog. Chewbacca shook his coat, raised his muzzle and pranced cheerfully. These two amazing dogs weren't the least discouraged by our circumstances and I wasn't going to disappoint them with my own misgivings. Perhaps there would be no layover in the storm after all. We were going home.

Returning to the sled, I released the snow hooks and the team began to pull slowly away. At the front of the team, I could just make out the shadowy forms of Zyphr and Chewbacca as they leaped and floundered while inching us forward through the drifting landscape. They seemed not the least bothered by the dismal conditions and amazed me with not only their endurance but their shear will and determination. In time, I was able to return the two rested dogs from the sled back into our team. This added a measure of encouragement to Chewbacca and Zyphr against their struggle in our uphill climb.

That night I learned what good lead dogs will do for you. Not because of what they have to do but because of what they *want* to do. Later that night, after pulling safely into camp, Chewbacca and Zyphr stood poised at the front of our team with wagging tails in a way that seemed to say, "Well, here we are safe and sound back at the truck. Let's Eat!" So sincere are they for their work that after a round of thankful hugs and hearty meals, my debt for their efforts was fully repaid. Given the opportunity to stretch their limitations, I had been taught another lesson about what these dogs can do.

Years later, when the dogs and I arrived in Alaska for the Serum Run '25 expedition, I was advised by a veteran musher, "Your dogs are capable of doing much more than you think they can." At the time, that advice seemed almost hard to believe. After all, I had been running my dogs for several years and thought by now I had gained a full understanding of each of them. But I was wrong. In Alaska we would be tested in ways I couldn't imagine. The lesson learned years earlier about what good dogs will do for you in a grim situation would be taught to me all over again - only in larger ways.

"Before the First Snow Flies"
With the passing of summer and the return of cooler temperatures, the dogs are anxious to hit the trail.
Training begins on unpaved mountain back roads several weeks prior to the first snowfall.
Gifford Pinchot National Forest

Training, Outfitting, and Fitful Sleep

"Go Confidently in the Direction of Your Dreams"

- Henry David Thoreau

August 15, 2008

I have always believed that the pursuit of dreams begins with a giant "leap of faith". On August 15th, my decision to apply for the 2009 Serum Run '25 expedition was published on our "Call of the Wild Huskies" website. While this commitment helped to stoke the fires of our early planning activities, ahead of us stretched a long string of threatening obstacles. These obstacles we nick-named "deal breakers". Failure to overcome any single one could potentially shut down weeks of planning, training, and money already spent.

"Summer Vacation is Over"
Some of Von's dogs dressed and ready for a fall training run.
From L to R are Birch, Cherry, Chewbacca, and Grits.

It is a long way to Nome. It is an even longer journey to prepare for, and arrive at, the expedition's point of departure. It can boggle the mind and it will test your nerves. Not only will it require many months of planning, training, and outfitting but it will be expensive.

Even when all is ready, with the gear packed and the dogs loaded on the truck, there remains the lonely three thousand mile midwinter drive to Alaska. Once there, several more weeks of training and the repacking of supplies for air drops by bush planes to checkpoints along the expedition route will be required. Then there is the final drive north with all the dogs, the sled, and gear to the railhead at Nenana.

The distance from the expedition's start at Nenana across ice covered tundra, lakes and marshes, down the lengths of solidly frozen rivers, and over mountain ranges to Nome is estimated at about 800 miles. No one knows for sure what the exact distance is. To this day no roadway connects the two.

It is a long way to Nome even when measured metaphorically. The years of experience on the trail including training and camping, dog care, navigation skills, and the knowledge that comes from working constantly in inclement weather, all of it can be measured as part of the distance to Nome. Yet from my earliest notion of driving a dog team across Alaska, it never entered my mind - not even as a passing thought - that we would fail to make our destination. Somehow I held the idea that once we left

Nenana things would take care of themselves. At the planning stage, a successful finish in Nome seemed to hinge on just getting to the start of the expedition. Once we "pulled hook", I imagined my dog team settling into the single cycle of running, eating, and resting. The many months of careful preparation and fretting over logistics would be left far behind. We were going to Nome. Or so I thought. For while I was well versed as to what to expect from an Alaskan winter, "Mother Nature" was already harboring secret plans, unknown to all, for the coming winter.

"Ham Tongues"
Team dogs Pike (L) and Willow (R) await a cool drink
after their first "dry land" conditioning run of the season
October 11, 2008

September 15th, 2009

After four weeks of preliminary planning, a family meeting is called. Proper preparation for the Serum Run expedition will require teamwork. The countless details which require attention are almost overwhelming. It is more than one person can manage - at least without losing your mind.

To begin with, the deadline to submit my application for the Serum Run'25 expedition is October 1st. Although the mushers selected for the expedition won't be announced until later that month, we are forced to begin our preparations in September. In the meantime, we can only hope our efforts will not be in vain.

Besides training the dogs, there are several weeks worth of meals to prepare in advance. What should the menu include and how will the food be packed? What kind of gear will the dogs and I need to survive long distance travel at forty or even fifty degrees below zero? Will my dogsled survive the rugged trail without being rebuilt? What will I do for a tent while camped on the Yukon River? And who will I find as a snow machine partner willing to help transport our expedition supplies clear across Alaska?

Near the top of the "to do" list are sewing protective booties to be worn by the dogs throughout the expedition. To help save cost, mom volunteers to undertake this mammoth task. To supply twelve huskies for at least nineteen days on the trail we will need at least one thousand five hundred booties. Each one of them must be hand cut and it will take many weeks bent over a sewing machine to complete them all.

September 25th, 2008

After weeks of mulling over my Serum Run '25 application, the many paged document is signed and mailed to Alaska. By now I am already feeling like there's "no turning back" even though I am only standing at the threshold of a roaring maelstrom of anticipation and anxiety. Although we do not expect the announcement of the candidates chosen for the expedition until mid October, we have no choice but to begin jumping over an endless road of hurdles stretching to the horizon.

Included in the Serum Run '25 expedition application is a sobering "Acknowledge of Risks" form to be signed and returned, addressing a host of dangers inherent to long distance travel by dog teams.

"These dangers may result in serious injury or death, and include but are not limited to attacks from wild animals, falling into a river, resulting in injury, drowning, or hypothermia, weather related injuries including hypothermia, acts of nature not limited to inclement weather, and equipment failure."

In early October I undergo an MRI on my knee for an old mushing injury, a full blown physical, and cardiovascular testing. Even though I am considered "fit" at fifty-six years of age, a hidden glitch in any single medical report could potentially ruin my chances for the expedition.

The MRI reveals a torn knee ligament and the orthopedic specialist warns that I could postpone corrective surgery if I take care not to suffer any serious falls. But falls while running dog teams are commonplace. They can involve twisting limbs, sharp blows, or worse. And it can happen more than once on any given day. Even though I know it will be unlikely, perhaps even impossible to avoid falls while training for and running in Alaska, I am willing to take my chances.

October 11th, 2008

Our first training runs of the season begin with a wheeled rig on rural forest roads. In a perfect world, we would have begun early morning runs in September. Even though the first snowfall is several weeks away, we begin with short conditioning runs in early October. These are run over dirt and gravel roads dusted with crisp autumn leaves. It is a beautiful time of year and the dogs are cheerful to hit the trail after their long "summer vacation".

"Muscling Up"
Tigger (L) and her brother Grits (R) lead a November training run while pulling a heavy wheeled rig
Gifford Pinchot National Forest

October 21st, 2008 - (e-mail correspondence from the Serum Run Selection Committee)

"Dear 2009 Serum Run Participants—

Congratulations! Are you ready for the trip of a lifetime and to be inundated with emails? Well I hope so, because you are embarking on probably one of the largest trips you will ever do in your life . . . Right now our group consists of eleven mushers, three alternates, and nineteen snowmachiners."

We are in! This is where the rubber hits the road. Every mile of training, every hour on the phone, and every minute spent attending to meticulous details has got to count. It is the beginning of fitful sleep and long days of hard work. And there will be no time off.

Proper training of the dogs is the single most important part of our numerous preparations. The entire success of our expedition hangs on the conditioning of our dogs for the long run across Alaska. Everything else, the purchase of new dog gear, the preparation of special meals for the dogs, even the sewing of the booties, none of it will matter if the dogs are not prepared to run upwards to fifty five miles a day for approximately nineteen days in sub-zero temperatures. Beginning with teams of only four dogs running three to five miles, we ramp up in a few short weeks to larger teams covering approximately fifteen miles. Copious notes are recorded for every run logged together with mileage, trail conditions, weather reports, and team positions for each dog.

November 2nd, 2008 - Training Log Entry

"*Leaders did not slow for fourteen miles. Cherry bleeding left front nail at twelve miles - bootied and OK. Pike held up well pulling off and on the last six miles. Feet OK. Teek displays left front pad soreness but legs OK. One hundred and eight miles logged to date.*"

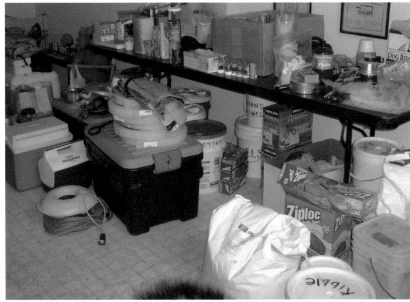

"The Supply Depot"
Countless expedition supplies clutter the kitchen while waiting to be sorted and carefully packed prior to departure for Alaska

In early November I receive the best news since my selection for the Serum Run expedition. My employer has agreed to grant me a sixty day sabbatical from work! A major "deal breaker" has been dodged. By late November many items critical to the expedition have also been ordered including a complete set of vaccines for the dogs from Nebraska, hardware from Los Angeles to make picket lines for our huskies, and furs from Montana to fabricate a ruff for my snowsuit.

In early December I receive an invitation from Jo and Ken Walch of Big Lake Alaska to be my host family while there. Jo has a kennel of seven huskies and is a recreational musher. There is a trail leading right out of their driveway down to a frozen lake where there are miles of training opportunities. It sounds just perfect. A major planning hurdle is checked off my list. In another big break, I learn that Phil Pryzmont, a commercial fisherman and back country travel guide from Nome Alaska, has agreed to be my snowmachine partner for the Serum Run '25 expedition. Check another major planning obstacle off the list.

In other big news, the arrangement for a driver to return my dog truck to the Anchorage area from Nenana and to help receive my dogs when airlifted out of Nome has been arranged. Judy Carrick, a long time mushing colleague recently relocated to Willow, Alaska, has agreed to volunteer for the job. Another "deal breaker" in our logistical planning is resolved. Providence seems to be showing the way.

In December we switch from our wheeled dry land training gig to a dog sled. It is a time of unsettled, transitional weather in the Washington Cascades and an almost unpredictable mixture of sleet, rain, and snow are hurled upon us. By mid December deep snow is already accumulating on our mountain trail systems.

December 15th, 2008 - Training Log Entry

"12 degrees Fahrenheit and breezy. Deep unbroken trail and rutted. Very good work by Chewbacca. Pike did very well and hard working on a tough trail. Sol-leks 'dolphining' in deep snow and tiring."

Due to a series of storms bringing dangerously high winds and deep snowfall to the Cascades, we begin to fall behind our targeted one thousand miles of training before February 22nd. On January 4th, 2009 we have logged only three hundred and eighty-three miles and the forced closure of many trail systems by Forest Service authorities continues to jeopardize our training schedule.

"Shakedown Training and Wild Wolves"
The dog teams of Von Martin (R), Margaret Black, and Don Duncan prepare for a three day training "shakedown" and campout near Elk River, Idaho. Due to sightings of large wolves in the area, the huskies were safely secured onboard the dog trucks each night.
January 17, 2009

January 13th, 2009 - Training Log Entry

"With only 18 days left for preparations prior to departure, our planning now shifts from frantic to near panic. There is still much left to do. Judy has just completed the 31 sealed and frozen dinners I'll require for the Serum Run Expedition and travel to Alaska and back. Next, she'll prepare the sealed breakfast meals and my midday snacks for the trail. How much freezer space is all this going to take?"

"By my estimate, the entire journey is going to require at least 800 lbs of the highest quality dog kibble. Besides packing the kibble on my little eight foot trailer, I'll need to leave room for ice chests to carry 120 lbs of meat diet for the dogs, another 50 lbs of frozen meat snacks for the dogs, and nearly 100 lbs of beef suet. How many ice chests is all this going to require? Will I be able to fit it all on the trailer?"

"My checklist is growing each day. Thank goodness for computers and spreadsheets. How did the early explorers manage doing all this with hand written ledgers? My respect for them is growing daily as I experience first hand the dizzying task of organizing supplies, and logistics for an expedition."

"Our goal to complete 1,500 booties for the dog team is well underway. Much of last week was spent on the phone ordering supplies and outfitting. There was that extra snow hook and line we are going to need to help set a picket line in camp. Also at least six more high test carabineers. Then there are the two pairs of arctic boots. There is the new pair of arctic mitts for driving the dog team at 40 below. How many chemical hand and foot warmers are we going to need? Better buy a few more boxes at Costco. We should take out shares of stock there."

"Our outfitting also required a new arctic sleeping bag rated at 60 below. There was the new 24 oz. ladle for dishing out the dog's food into bowls while in camps and cans of Gold Bonds Powder for the dog's feet."

In a strategic move to step up our training program and meet the Serum Run organizer's

"Camp Von - Vaughan"
An Arctic Oven tent complete with wood stove is established at the Serum Run '25 shakedown base camp near Elk River, Idaho

"Breakfast on Ice"
Von's training day begins with hot coffee and a hearty breakfast of potatoes, bell peppers, onions, and scrambled eggs topped with cheese and served up in a metal dog food bowl

requirement of a "Shakedown Run", fellow Serum Run '25 expedition mushers Don Duncan and Margaret Black organize a three day training run and campout near Elk River, Idaho where better trail conditions have been reported.

Jan 17th, 2009 - Training Log Entry

"On the way into Elk River for our "shakedown" run with Margaret and Don. It's a seven hour drive to Margaret's house where I layover for the night before heading on to Elk River. Once there, we'll meet up with Don . . . set up our base camp, and begin our three days of running."

The purpose of the shakedown run is to replicate, as closely as possible, our Serum Run mushing experience in Alaska. Every piece of gear and clothing must be put to the test. All meals are taken in camp, arctic sleeping bags will provide our bedding, and multiple runs for our dog teams of thirty five miles or more will be planned. After establishing our base camp near Elk River, we are advised by locals of several large wolves scouring the area. Although the dogs are normally bedded on straw along a 50' picket line, it is decided to bed them onboard the dog trucks each night to avoid the risk of attack by marauding wolves.

The weather is glorious, sunny and clear with subzero night-time temperatures and daytime highs in the low twenty's. The hard trail makes for snappy runs and all is well until we crest a steep mountain pass during a long training run on our second day. Don had warned us about a series of perilously tight switchbacks we would encounter on the back side of the pass.

As a measure of safety, it is decided to space the teams well apart in case anyone looses control of their team or suffers a fall on the way down the mountain. By mutual agreement, I will take the lead and be ready to assist either team following behind if necessary. But things don't go as planned.

Almost immediately after cresting the pass, my team is pitched into a steep downhill plunge. In just seconds the dogs are at a full run. Even with both feet planted firmly on the sled brake, it has little effect on our downhill fall and the first of several frightening switchbacks appears almost instantaneously into view. I'm already having doubts about a clean downhill run but there is little time think about that now.

Leaning sharply into the turn, I wrestle the

"Bacon and Grits"
Twin brothers Bacon (L) and Grits (R) finish their trail snacks during a "shakedown" training run near Elk River, Idaho

sled's driving bow with all the shoulder I've got. But the dogs, insane with their downhill speed, are oblivious to my struggle to control the sled and reach for all the speed they can make. Like a game of "crack the whip" gone out of control, the sled goes airborne, rolling to the right before crashing down on the ice paved trail.

The sled rolls two or three times and suddenly I'm aware of being dragged on my back while holding onto the sled with a one handed death grip. My first thought goes to the danger of the sharp snow hooks that have been ejected from their holsters and are bouncing across the ice just inches away.

My next thought goes to the dogs. With no braking to slow their descent, and more dangerous switchbacks ahead, they could become entangled in their own lines and injured. Even though it doesn't seem possible, the sled continues to pick up speed as I'm dragged like useless garbage upside down behind the sled. It is little use to call out to the dogs who are now totally insane with their full throttle flight down the mountain.

It's not the first time I have found myself in this situation but somehow I had always managed to hang on, to stay with the sled until the team finally slowed and I could regain my mount. In all my years on a sled, I have never lost my team. Now that is all about to

"Brothers"
Brothers Boomer (L) and Patrick (R), the most powerful dogs on the team, run in "wheel position" immediately in front of the sled
Elk River, Idaho

change. One by one, my fingers are wretched from the sled like some invisible giant hand prying them away. My grip is reduced to just three fingers, then only two. With a snap, my grip is finally wretched loose and I skid to a halt half buried in the snow. I roll over onto my stomach just in time to see the dogs round a sharp turn to the right and disappear from view. I have lost my team.

I give little thought to the fact that I'm stranded half a day's run from our camp, or that I had just passed the fresh tracks of a very large wolf less than a mile back on the trail. I can only think about my dogs and how fearful I am for their safety. There are many dangers presented to a team on an unbridled run down a winding mountain trail. Legs could become entangled, tearing ligaments or much worse. The dogs could ball up in a terrible tangle and a fight could break out. It is a musher's worst possible nightmare.

In seconds, I am on my feet and making the best speed I can in a downhill sprint in pursuit of my team. It is difficult going in heavy snow boots and in spite of the cold temperatures, I break out quickly in a uneasy, clammy sweat. Suddenly from behind, I hear the cries of Margaret driving her team of Siberian Huskies as they beautifully burst through the sharp turn and bolt past me. Seconds later, Don and his team of Sammy's fly past me and disappear around the next turn. Will they see my dogs ahead of them in time to avoid a collision? Will they become entangled with my own dog team on the way down the mountain?

After several heart pounding minutes, I come upon my team sprawled at the edge of the trail in a mess of tangled tuglines and chewed necklines. Amazingly, one of the snow hooks that had been flailing fearfully close to the sled had hooked on a snag and miraculously held, bringing the entire team to a halt. They were still panting madly and watched me trot up to them while their tongues lolled from wide grinning faces. Checking each dog for injury, I set about untangling lines and restoring order to the team. They were safe. Or so I thought. For sports injuries suffered by sled dogs are not always immediately apparent and the shadow of a disguised injury would later follow us all the way to Alaska.

"The Long Dog Train"
Boomer looks back from Von's team during a snack break for the dogs on a thirty-five mile training run with the teams of Margaret Black and Don Duncan

January 26th, 2009 - Training Log Entry

"Just completed our last two days of training prior to our departure to Alaska. On Sunday, I hooked up all twelve for the first time and ran twenty-three miles with a few incidents . . . Had a couple of bad tangles but we did alright . . . Sol-leks came up a little lame in his left rear leg. Five days to go until our departure . . . just a few days to finish sorting and wrapping up details on the home front with family and finances and then we'll be on our way . . ."

With nearly all our plans in place, and just days remaining to organize and load 1,200 pounds of supplies onto the truck and trailer, I turn my attention to the fulfillment of a four year old promise. Taking Wolfie's tin of ashes from its place in the cabin, I bolt her old dog tag to the front of the round, four pound tin that contains her remains. "Wolfie Martin - Lead Dog" her tag reads. To guard the precious cargo against the eight hundred mile ride across Alaska by dog sled, I pack her tin inside two heavy zip lock freezer bags.

Before carrying her out to the dog truck, my eyes catch sight of her dog collar looped over her portrait above the fireplace. Removing it from the its place, I shove it into my pocket just for good luck. In a few days we will be on our way. I am as ready as I can be.

"Wolfie," I mutter aloud, "we're going to Nome girl."

"Gateway to Alaska"
A glistening sheet of blue-white ice paves the Alaskan Highway as it enters the Alaskan Range
from the Yukon Territory. This final leg of the journey to Alaska between Tok and Big Lake
covered more than 350 twisting, mountainous miles as temperatures plunged to 18 degrees below zero

North to Alaska

"The pitiless expanse of the Great White Silence"

- Jack London

February 1st, 2009 - Serum Run Log

"We left for Alaska today. It was a rather tearful departure, not for myself, but for the dogs who didn't get to go. I want to talk about Teek . . . he really wanted to go. Sol-leks revealed a leg injury on the last day of training. He is being treated and recovering slowly but surely. An examination by the vet shows he should be OK for the start of the Serum Run."

"But just before leaving, Sol-leks laid on the porch while Teek pounded on his kennel and gave me a big smile like he just knew I was going to take him . . . but I can't take them all."

"It was a long day of packing until 1:00 am Sunday morning. We finally got underway at 11:19 am. It was a long uneventful drive up to the border crossing. Then a longer drive into Canada, dropping the dogs every three hours on the way up. Got north of Hope and learned that the drive is a little miserable . . . one hundred miles of narrow canyons with gusty winds and icy patches. No place to be driving at night and no welcome into Canada. After traveling for twelve hours I got the dogs out. It was extremely windy with drifting snow but got them fed. They were happy to get their food."

"Wind, Snow and Ice"
Boomer, Pike, Sol-leks, and Cherry seek shelter under the truck from a snowstorm near the Trans-Canadian Highway. Throughout the long drive to Alaska, it was necessary to remove the dogs from their boxes every three hours of travel.

February 2nd, 2009 - Serum Run Log

"Drove over Quesnel, it was very deep in snow. Dropped down off that mountain and right back over another one before arriving at Dawson Creek which leads you into Fort St. John - a grimy town that doesn't display itself as a 'white wonderland'. This area is dominated by trucks and you provide them every opportunity to pass you by. There are few automobiles. The dogs are doing pretty well and thirsty most of the time. Grits is not eating well."

February 3rd, 2009 - Serum Run Log

"Hours driven since leaving home - 22 hours and 40 minutes . . . total miles traveled, 990 miles. One of the challenges is keeping up with water for the dogs due to water freezing overnight. Most of the drive through British Columbia is mountainous and challenging to your driving skills. The dogs do not draw much attention here except for occasional waves from passing truckers. I have been making

"Dog Camp in the Canadian Rockies"
Some of Von's sled dogs enjoy time off of the truck following a snowstorm on the Trans-Canadian Highway,
deep in the Canadian Rockies. From L to R are Bacon, Tigger, Birch, Grits, Chewbacca, and Patrick.

long days on the road averaging 12 hours and the best possible progress while there are no storms
blowing. Saw a silver fox run off with a road kill. The dogs are getting pretty fat."

"9:17 pm - I am camped about 6 hours northwest of Fort Nelson - right in the middle of the North
Canadian Rockies at a very foreboding place. The drive through the Rockies is interesting - it began to
snow very hard. Had extremely high winds gusting to 60 mph but still cooked for all the dogs - bundled
up and went about my business in the dark working by the light of the half moon. Got all the dogs fed
as they sat with their backs to fierce winds that didn't seem to bother Bacon at all . . . or Blackjack."

February 4th, 2009 - Serum Run Log

"Arose early from our campout high in the Canadian Rockies near Lake Concho. It is a beautiful
morning and offers a breathtaking view. There is absolutely no sound here at all. I'm looking east
across a long valley and in every direction the mountains rise jaggedly against the skyline. It is a mag-

"Dog Drop in the Yukon Territory"
Von's huskies stretch their legs at twenty-two degrees below zero under deep blue sunny skies.
The drive to Alaska covered over 2,500 miles and required travel up to fourteen hours a day for six days.

nificent and frightful place. It is a huge land. If you imagine folks in their cozy city homes being plucked out and put down into a place like this, it couldn't help but completely change who you think you are - your place on this earth - how magnificent and big it is - and how small our own worlds' really are. The dogs were howling during the middle of the night and I wasn't too excited about them possibly attracting wild animals to the truck."

Fortunately, the worst of yesterday's heavy snowfall is plowed from the highway during the early morning hours. As we continue our drive, numerous signs appear warning of wild buffalo herds on the roadway.

"10:05 am - just passed a huge herd of buffalo . . . they're looking over at me. Never seen anything as big as these guys . . . there they are, ambling along. We've got a big herd in the road. They're across the road and now I'm stopping. There's probably twenty of them across the road. They are wandering towards my dog truck. Now they are just a foot or two away. The dogs are barking at them and

"The Road to Destruction Bay"

An arrow straight section of the Trans-Canadian Highway cuts through the frozen Yukon Territory on its icy rendezvous with Destruction Bay

they're just looking at us. They're a little curious about the dogs. I can hear Cherry barking at them and now they're only inches away . . ."

I'm eyeball to eyeball with a huge buffalo brushing past the driver's door. My huskies launch into a screaming chorus from their dog boxes and I can't be sure what will happen next. The herd is blocking the road in front of us and several more surround us on each side. Their enormous wooly heads brush past the huskies' kennels who are insane from the sight and smell of them. Amazingly, the buffalo show little interest in the dogs, and I am glad when they wander off and we are safely on our way.

"At about 1:00 pm we crossed over into the Yukon Territory. I haven't seen Sgt. Preston or his huskies yet, but Sol-leks and Pike are on the lookout for him . . ."

Shortly before 9:00 pm we arrive safely in Whitehorse as the temperature drops to 15 degrees below zero. The dogs all come out at our roadside camp to enjoy a good hot meal before returning their cozy straw filled dog boxes. Once they are settled, I do my best to sleep curled in the back of the truck clutching a pair of chemical hand warmers. But the dogs cry on and off until dawn and I'm up half a dozen times to look after them. It makes for a long cold night.

February 5th, 2009 - Serum Run Log

"It is 12:54 pm and the temperature is eight degrees below zero. I am currently skirting Destruction Bay with the dogs in tow. It brings to mind Antarctica. There's a large frozen bay and mountain ranges rising from all sides that are ice covered and treeless."

"Blue skies rise above vistas that allow the eye to travel across the landscape for nearly a hundred miles. It's absolutely breathtaking. I'm reminded of

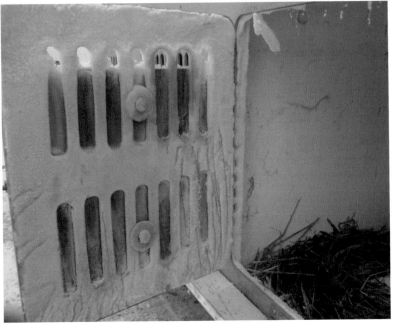

"Sled Dog Ice Box"

At twenty-four degrees below zero, the dog's exhaled breath condenses, forming growing layers of ice on the inside of their straw fill dog boxes

"An Antarctic-like Landscape"
One of the most remote and unforgiving places on earth, a breakdown at the edge of solidly frozen
Destruction Bay in the Yukon Territory could prove fatal without proper outfitting. Von and his
huskies made the long drive to Alaska loaded with more than 1,200 lbs of food and supplies

an Ansel Adams painting with the moon rising a few degrees above the horizon. It's the stuff that art-ists dream of. A wolf crossed the road right in front of me . . . I just missed him . . . he crossed over and shot a look back at the dogs on the truck."

"5:42 pm . . . We are safely in Alaska. The temperature is 14 degrees below zero. Miles traveled since leaving home are 2,137. It is dusk and the sun is setting over the mountain range. It is good to be here."

February 6th, 2009 - Serum Run Log

"10:30 am and 16 degrees below zero. Leaving Tok, Alaska. It's still over 300 miles to our final destination at Big Lake - so still a very long drive ahead and also the Alaska Range to cross. Tigger was real cold so she is riding with her brother today. That should offer her a little cheer . . . she seems a little down in the mouth and didn't want to eat this morning. I should have put her in with Grits yes-terday on that last leg of the Yukon where it was 24 degrees below zero in the daytime."

"Ready Whenever You Are"
Grits, one of three Command Leaders for Von's expedition team,
sits ready in harness and booties for his first training run in Alaska
February 11th, 2009

Drop Bags and a Trip to the Vet

"The dog is the most faithful of animals"

- Martin Luther

"Drop Bag Contents"
Dozens of "coded" bags containing food, drink, and miscellaneous supplies are sorted prior to being delivered by air cargo to six points along the 800 mile expedition route

Early in the evening of February 6th, the huskies and I arrive, "dog tired", at the home of our host family, Jo and Ken Walch, in Big Lake, Alaska. It is a beautiful location situated on a low forested hill overlooking a moonlit lake. Jo's outdoor kennel of Siberian Huskies are among the first to welcome us, and a stirring "call of the wild" is exchanged between all the dogs as we pull in well after dark.

After looking after my dogs, Jo and Ken graciously show me to a cozy, private apartment with a window view across the lake. I have been traveling, eating, and camping in the same clothes for six days. It is good to freshen up and shake off the road, but mostly I want sleep. At the same time, I am not unaware of the fact that travel on the expedition by dog team is going to make the last six days in the truck look like a vacation.

February 10th, 2009 - Serum Run Log

"It's 7:47 am from Big Lake, Alaska where the temperature is 18 degrees below zero. The skies are clear and a big, beautiful full moon is just setting over the lake to the west. Completed my drop bags and loaded them onto the truck last night at 11:00 pm. Afterwards, I was dead tired. It's been several days of sorting, packing, and getting settled in with my host family who have graciously opened their home to me during my stay in Alaska."

"Some of the dogs are having a little trouble adjusting to the cold temperatures. Grits has not eaten well in several days. But most of the dogs seem happy and Tigger has bounced back and now eating very well. Chewy has taken control of things and showing everyone he's the boss and never bothered by the weather. Jack is having a good time - nothing seems to bother that dog one bit. Bacon, the dog I was most concerned about on this trip, is eating voraciously and jumping around all the time. I'm pleased to see that he is looking so strong. Pike is having the time of his life. Sol-leks is kinda quiet."

"Yesterday Don, Margaret, and I loaded straw (for the dogs) into a rented U-Haul truck. Today it will be taken to the airport, together with our drop bags for shipment by air cargo to points along the

"Fare Fit For a King"
Tasty precooked meals for more than nineteen days
are sorted on the snow prior to repacking into drop bags

Photo credit Ken Walch

"Fit to Be Tied"
Von Martin works to "fid" each of his thirty expedition
drop bags closed with a small poly rope prior to shipment
by air cargo service to points along the expedition route

expedition route. It's been very cold everyday. My head has been spinning and the days pass quickly."

"After working outside at 15 degrees below zero to close up drop bags, I went inside, flopped on the floor, and passed out fully dressed. It's a hearty cycle of work in the cold and eating when you can."

Our drop bags are the lifeline of the expedition. Their carefully inventoried contents contain absolutely everything the dogs and I will need for at least 19 days on the trail between Nenana and Nome. There is little chance of making up shortages in route, and every imaginable need, other than what is carried on the sled, must be packed and shipped out on the trail.

Included in my own drop bags are over four hundred pounds of dog kibble, individually packaged in twenty pound bags. There is more than one hundred pounds of meat and snacks to nourish the dogs during breaks along the trail. There are more than a thousand booties for the dogs, neatly packed into zip lock freezer bags. I have also planned for every meal, snack, and drink I will require for the 800 mile backcountry journey. There are extra batteries for my headlamp, socks and replacement liners for my boots. Even fire logs for the tent stove have been carefully measured out and bagged. Nothing can be overlooked.

In my dog sled will be packed tools and supplies essential to sled repairs, sleeping bag, food for myself and the dogs, a cooker, a cooler for mixing kibble, snowshoes, ski poles, and an extra parka, hats and gloves. The list goes on and on. It must all somehow fit in the sled to be hauled all the way to Nome by my twelve best canine buddies. Last but not least, I have reserved a special spot at the front of the sled to carry Wolfie's little four pound tin of ashes.

"1:46 pm - just completed loading all the drop bags at the air cargo warehouse. What a job that was! The straw had to be bagged, palletized, and shrink wrapped. The team's drop bags had to be

"Drop Bag Day"
Thousand of pounds of expedition supplies and straw bedding for the dogs are sorted and assembled on pallets after being weighed and tagged at an Anchorage air freight warehouse. Each bag is individually labeled with the name of the expedition team member and its drop point destination along the 800 mile route

individually weighed, tagged, palletized, and shrink wrapped as well. It took about four and a half hours to get through the whole process."

"Tomorrow morning Don, Margaret, and I will do our first runs with our dogs out of Willow where the Iditarod restart takes place. We will probably run six-dog teams to hold down speed and power because the dogs haven't run in over two weeks and we want them to stretch out on the trail and get their legs back."

With straw for the dogs and drop bags delivered to air cargo in Anchorage, our attention shifts to training the dogs and preparing for our final drive north to Nenana. It is just twelve days until our departure from the railhead at Nenana.

"The Call of the Wild"
Petite little Cherry, one of Von's Alaskan Huskies, raises her voice in song while awaiting a training run with the dog team

photo credit Ken Walch

"Pike the Lion Hearted"
Expressing patience with warm, hopeful eyes, Pike, one of Von's Siberian Huskies, awaits
"hookup" on his first day of Alaskan training with the Serum Run '25 expedition team
Willow, Alaska

February 12th, 2009 - Serum Run Log

"Yesterday was the first run in Alaska with my own dogs which made it very special. From the recreation center at Willow, we ran the dogs right down onto the lake."

The area is dotted with residences where plowed roadways occasionally intersect the dog trails. It is here that we have our first bit of trouble in Alaska. After running over the lake, we cross a couple of frozen sloughs, then over another lake before entering the woods. Further on, a small snow berm across the trail marks the spot where a plowed roadway intersects our path. Without hesitation, Chewy and Grits climb the small berm and confidently enter the intersection. It is probably thirty feet across the plowed gravel road to where the dog trail picks up on the other side. Then the dogs stop. For a moment, Chewy and Grits look at each another as if they are working out a secret plan.

"Frozen Lake Crossing"
Lead dogs Chewbacca (L) and Grits (R), pause during a training run as mushers Margaret Black
and Don Duncan consult map coordinates from their dogsleds during a frozen lake crossing.
February 11th, 2009

Without warning, they turn sharply left and break into a full gallop, dragging the team and sled in tow. I immediately recognize their reasoning. "Why should we run down that narrow dog trail," they probably thought, "when there is this nice wide one here instead?" It is only my first hour on the trail in Alaska and already I have become separated from the other teams and running completely in the wrong direction. But the dogs love it. We fly around a turn in the road and I look back just in time to see the teams of Don and Margaret disappearing from view. The sled brake offers little help against the smooth icy roadway and there is no way to set a snow hook. I have no idea how far we might travel like this.

Along each side of the road, the snow is piled two feet high from plowing. After wrestling the sled towards the shoulder a foot at a time, I reach out to set a hook in the firmly packed snow. Our stop is almost instantaneous, causing my stomach to meet sharply against the sled's driving bow. Running forward, I grab Chewy and Grits by the neckline and lead them in a wide circle back in the opposite direc-

49

tion. Before I can remount the sled, they swing back the other way and pop the snow hook. Catching the sled just in time, I'm jerked off my feet but hold on. I'm not going to loose my team - not on our first day in Alaska.

After a few more failed attempts to turn the team around, Chewy and Grits surrender their idea of a run on the wide trail to nowhere and agree to turn back. Many minutes later, we arrive at the intersection leading to the dog trail and are safely on our way. Later that day I record the highlights of our first two training runs in Alaska.

"We got onto a nice trail system and only saw one snowmachine during the run. There were a couple of road crossings that are interesting when you go the wrong way. Pike thoroughly enjoyed the run and pulled the whole time . . . the dogs all had a great time."

"On the second run with Tigger and Bacon in the lead, we followed Margaret and Don across the lake and back into the woods. Then Don signaled me to stop and gave the turn around quick sign. There was a moose on the trail coming right at us! We didn't want to share the trail with him on our first day out, so we did our U-turns and beat it back to the dog trucks. All the dogs did fine."

"No Lookin' Back Now"
Boomer (L) and Pike (R), look back at the dog team driven by Margaret Black
during a break on the inaugural training run near Willow, Alaska
February 11th, 2009

February 14, 2009 - Serum Run Log

"Yesterday, after a short run with Sol-leks in the team, I came to the conclusion that his leg has not improved. I have been forced into the hard decision to drop him from the expedition. It came not without a few tears. Sol-leks is the first dog that I thought would get to Nome and this is a real blow. I have to set my emotions aside and do what is best for him. Still, I'm going to miss him terribly."

"Right now my focus is on running the dogs and watching every detail about them . . . how they are eating, how they're moving on the trail, how they recover, and how they are handling the weather. They are the common denominator and the bottom line to what stands between Nenana and Nome. It's really up to them."

"For the last two days I have been training on Big Lake with six dog squads. Pike looks really good. This evening when returning after dark, we got into a bad tangle and there was a nasty alteration between the dogs but no injuries. Temperatures have been warm. It climbed to 38 degrees today, so we hope it cools a bit. It's pretty warm for the dogs."

Photo credit Ken Walch

"A Sad Day for Sol-leks"
In a heartbreaking decision, Von is forced to withdraw Sol-leks from the run to Nome after a second examination by specialist reveals a torn ligament in his left knee. While always making the best decisions for his dogs, Von tearfully tell Sol-leks, "I'm gonna miss you terribly."

February 15th, 2009 - Serum Run Log

"We've had a warm front move into the area with the lows remaining above freezing. I'll have to hold back speeds and watch the heavier coated dogs. My biggest concern at this point are dogs not eating. I've got some good eaters. I've got Grits who is eating very poorly and loosing weight. He seems happy and healthy but has a very poor appetite. He will eat a little meat and dog biscuits only. He will barely touch his kibble at all. The weight looks good on every dog except Grits."

"Sol-leks has an appointment with the vet on Tuesday for an evaluation of his knee. Jo and Ken Walch have agreed to look after him while I am away. God willing, all eleven of my dogs will arrive safely in Nome."

February 16th, 2009 - Serum Run Log

"I am on my way to Jamie West's with all the dogs for training on her trails with Don and Margaret's teams. Afterwards, a group dinner is planned. All the dogs (are) still eating well except for Grits who would not eat breakfast and is now light as a feather. Jack just sniffed around his food but when I went to take it away, he pounded it like it was his last meal. Birch is a little lean but doing OK. Each day I have been massaging most of the dogs with Algyval ointment to relieve sore joints."

51

"Temperatures have been very warm in the Anchorage area. I understand temperatures in Nenana are running at about plus 10 degrees. Our first couple of days on the trail out of Nenana may be mild, even at 10 degrees. I expect some nice runs at those temps. I sure hope we can avoid the minus 35 to 50 degree temperatures as long as possible."

"All the dogs look really good in harness. Bacon is having a few issues with Patrick right now so we are working on those politics. I also tried Willow up front with Grits and had great results with that combination. If I can just get Grits eating, I will feel a lot better. I've never seen him go this long without food. I'm going to have the vet take a look at him . . ."

"Judy has been working with Alaska Airlines. There is still the possibility that Teek may come out. My concern is his weight is sixty-one pounds which is about ten pounds more than I would like him to be. Secondly, I am concerned about his lack of conditioning. But he has the "head" to go, the feet to go, and the coat to go."

"Boot Scootin' Boogie"
Some of the dogs bootied and ready to be hitched to the dog sled tethered at right.
From left to right are Boomer, Pike, and Grits

"The Final Countdown"
Von's huskies, lead by Tigger and Chewbacca, pull steadily in harness behind the teams of
Don Duncan and Margaret Black under overcast skies during one of their final training runs

Our group dinner at the home of veteran Serum Run '25 musher Jamie West, includes several mushers from the area. Jamie lives in a beautiful log home and Jo Walch provides a *very* hearty beef stew which is enjoyed by all. It is a warm gathering with lots of talk about mushing and the Serum Run trail. Jamie West spoke very highly of Phil Pryzmont, my snow machine partner for the expedition.

On Wednesday, I took Sol-leks and Grits to the vet and received some very unhappy news. Sol-leks was diagnosed by an expert sled dog veterinarian with a cruciate ligament tear, which means, for all purposes, that his running career is finished. Not only will Sol-leks be absent from our run to Nome, but he may never run in harness again. It is very sad news for my little "Daddy's Boy", but I am encouraged to learn that future surgery can restore his ability get around without a crippling knee.

The news about Grits is better and the vet says he is in really good shape! I am told he will not starve himself to death, although he may get thinner before our arrival in Nome. I am encouraged when the vet assures me Grits appetite will only be peaked once we increase our runs to more than fifteen miles a day.

"Escape from a Moose"
Bacon and Tigger, followed by Willow, Birch, Patrick, and Blackjack, beat
a hasty retreat across a frozen lake after being chased from the woods by a moose
Willow. Alaska

Teek to the Rescue

"Teek, who had not traveled so far that winter . . ."

- Jack London quote from Call of the Wild

February 17th, 2009 - Serum Run Log

"It is 8:17 pm, and I am on my way into Anchorage to pick up Teek! Is he ever going to be surprised to see everybody. He's not going to know where he is - but tomorrow he will when he is running across Big Lake. I'm really looking forward to seeing him."

"A Howling Good Time"
Teek prepares for his first Alaskan run following his overnight shipment by air cargo to replace Sol-leks on the team. Although deficient in training and conditioning, Teek's enthusiasm and steady strength added solidly to the team
February 18th, 2009

After three days of persistent phone calls to Alaska Airlines, Judy is able to successfully negotiate a great price for Teek's shipment by air freight from Seattle to Anchorage. The folks at Alaska Air Cargo are to be thanked for recognizing Teek's valuable role with a great icon of Alaskan heritage, the Serum Run '25 expedition. Our twelve dog team is complete!

February 18th, 2009 - Serum Run Log

"On my way in the truck to the south end of Big Lake and in the first team I am going to put Teak. If he looks good I'm going to run him sixteen miles. He seems very active, very happy . . . his weight is a little high but his agility seems good. I trimmed his feet this morning. His feet are a little splayed, so I will bootie him everyday on every foot."

"I Want Out"

Pike waits to be removed from the his kennel on the dog truck for another training run across Big Lake

"Taking care of these dogs is a never ending cycle. It's a full time job being on the road with twelve or thirteen huskies. It's a constant round of feeding dogs, cleaning bowls, scooping poop, getting lines in and out, getting the dogs on and off the truck, cleaning out the boxes, opening a new bale of straw, and on and on. Then there is the weather that you are always working against and it slows you down everywhere you go."

"Sol-lek's new dog house is almost done. The Walch's needed two new dog houses anyway and one of them will be Sol-leks while I away. Today Boomer chewed through his harness."

On Friday morning, February 21st, I rise early to feed the dogs and load the dog truck with the last of our supplies. The time has arrived and today will be driving north to Nenana. I am joined by long-time friend, and mushing colleague, Judy Carrick, who has generously volunteered to return my dog truck to Big Lake after the start of the expedition tomorrow. It will be a very long drive for her. Judy Carrick has ten Samoyeds of her own, so we are taking them along as well. At the moment my dog truck is bursting with expedition supplies, my dog sled, and twenty-two dogs!

Before departing Big Lake, I bid a sad farewell to Sol-leks. He knows the truck is loaded with all the gear and the dogs and I'm fighting back tears as he begs to go along. "Be good for Ken and Jo," I tell him. "I'll be back for you Sol-leks, I promise." I give him a parting kiss on his muzzle and manage a quick exit without a single look back. I can still feel his eyes on me as he follows my departure down the long driveway and disappear from view.

February 21st, 2009 - Serum Run Log

"2:05 pm - temperature 10 degrees - we are pulled to the side of the road in Cantwell. As we were fueling up, I noticed Don had another broken leaf spring on his trailer. So we're busting out our tools,

"Big Lake Reunion"
Running partners, Teek (L) and Pike (R), run side by side in wheel position during a
crossing of Big Lake. While training on the lake, Von's team shared the "road" with
snowmobiles, cars, trucks, and even a caravan of fully loaded cement mixers

"Roadside Repairs"
Serum Run musher Don Duncan (right foreground), is assisted by members of the expedition team,
including musher coordinator, Erin McLarnon (far left), Margaret Black and Judy Carrick (left center),
Von Martin (center), and team veterinarian, Dr Jerry Vanek (right center). The broken leaf spring
was repaired on the trailer near Denali National Park in route to Nenana, Alaska

getting down on our knees, and getting that "bad boy" changed out with an old extra spring he has onboard. I've got twenty-two dogs on the truck. My twelve plus Judy Carrick's ten Samoyeds. The drive has been beautiful all the way from Willow. It is a spectacular, sunny drive watching the Alaska Range. We had hoped to be in Nenana by 4:00 pm. It will probably be later now . . ."

After completing repairs to Don's dog trailer, we are on our way. The delay has cost us much time and our arrival in Nenana is delayed until dusk. We are greeted by strong winds and cold temperatures. There is a glorious display of the Northern Lights as I go about caring for my dogs on the truck. Suddenly my cheer is dampened with the receipt of terrible news. Phil Pryzmont, my snow machine partner for the Serum Run, has been missing for three days in a severe storm along the Kaltag portage. Phil had planned to drive his snowmachine, traveling alone from Nome to Nenana, a trip he has made sev-

"Judy Carrick's Sammys"
Willow musher, Judy Carrick, prepares to reload one of her ten Samoyeds after a offering them a drink and time off the truck. With no one to look after her dogs at home, Judy's Sammys' joined Von's huskies for the long drive north to Nenana

"Topping Off the Tank"
Von is joined by mushing colleague, Judy Carrick, who cheerfully volunteers to return his dog truck to Big Lake after the start of the expedition in Nenana

eral times in the past. But no one has heard from him since Wednesday and I'm told that there is a search on for him. I am encouraged with the knowledge that Phil is not only one of the best backcountry guides out of Nome, but he is well equipped for the journey. Still, his safety and whereabouts weighs heavily on my mind.

In the meantime, I have no one to haul my supplies to Nome, and the launch of the expedition is only hours away. My dogs and I have come so far just to get to the start at Nenana and I cannot allow myself to flounder in the depths of despair.

In darkness, I go earnestly about the business of preparing my sled for departure and to double check all the gear. As an astral display of Northern Lights shimmer overhead, gale force winds begin to build, buffeting my dogs picketed along a makeshift line strung between the truck and a nearby telephone pole. I move among the dogs, petting each of them and stoking their ears. "It's okay", I encourage them, "we'll find a way through this."

But Phil's disappearance is but one thread in a tapestry of bad fortune about to befall our expedition. Fate already lurks in the shadows guided by a full hand of misfortune that will soon dealt bad luck not only to our dogs, our snowmachines, and several of the team members, but will deliver us calamitous weather and a trail from hell.

Photo credit Judy Carrick

"Bring It On"
Von Martin stands ready at the Nenana Railroad Depot near the exact spot where the first relay musher,
"Wild Bill" Shannon, received the Diphtheria anti toxin by railway from Anchorage on January 27, 1925
February 22nd, 2009

Nenana Departure

"I take no credit - that goes only to the dogs"

- Wild Bill Shannon - 1925 Serum Run Musher

Von Martin and principal lead dog Chewbacca minutes before the expedition's departure from Nenana

Photo credit Judy Carrick

At 5:30 am on February 22nd, our team of mushers and snow machiners are aroused from our sleep in the community center. Throughout the night, gale force winds rocked the building, making for a restless night. Thankfully, the winds begin to diminish by the first light of day as we quickly pack our bedding and I see to my dogs outdoors. They are anxious to come off the truck and somehow sense there is something very special about this day. As I remove each dog from the truck, I tell them to bid farewell to their cozy, warm homes out of the wind. From here on, it will be outdoor living all the way to Nome.

Last night at 8:00 pm, the entire expedition team was assembled for a group meeting. It is our first assembly of eleven snow machiners and eight mushers. From this moment, we are our own community and will rely on one another for at least the next nineteen days. The welfare and safety of ourselves and the dogs will depend on our ability to work together as a team and look out for each other.

At breakfast I am introduced to Amy Whisler, an Anchorage pharmacist, who is a member of our medical mission team. Amy has agreed to substitute as my snow machine partner in lieu of Phil Pryzmont who remains missing somewhere along the Kaltag portage. At our first meeting near the truck, we have little time to discuss the organization and packing of my expedition supplies onto Amy's sled. Each snowmachiner on the expedition will be hauling a cargo sled, carefully packed, and hitched behind their snowmobile. Most of the snowmobiles are newer, powerful models set up for Alaska's back country travel. Still, the contents of the combined expedition supplies for both machiner and musher can total several hundred pounds. And it makes for a very heavy load.

Photo credit Evie Wakulenko

Amy Whisler, medical team specialist, meets with Von shortly before departure from Nenana to discuss packing strategy. Amy volunteered to substitute as Von's snowmachine partner for the Serum Run Expedition

"Serum Arrival"
At approximately 10:30 am, an Alaska Railroad train bearing the "Serum", is welcomed by the expedition team in Nenana

"Medical Mission Team"
The Serum Run '25 team of medical specialists before our departure from Nenana. (L to R) Amy Whisler, pharmacist; Dr. Brian Trimble, physician; Leslie Stephens, RN; and Evelyn "Evie" Wakulenko, RN

At first Amy cannot be sure what to expect from our new found partnership and neither can I. In the meantime, I offer her assurance that everything is going to work out just fine. I introduce her to all the dogs and encourage her to ask questions whenever she feels the need. Minutes before our departure from Nenana, I'm invited by Amy to review her rig all packed and ready to go. I'm impressed. Amy has done a first rate job loading, covering, and cinching down all of our supplies. Perhaps things are going to work out after all.

February 22nd, 2009 - Serum Run Log

"10:30 am - temperature 5 degrees - I am at the Nenana railway depot and the train is arriving in moments. The sled is packed, I've met my snowmachiner, and we are gathering at the (railway) station. We'll be hearing the train whistle blow in a moment. The conductor will hand off the (ceremonial) Serum packet which will be passed down the line of mushers and onto the sled of our honorary musher for the first leg into Old Minto."

"We have just passed the "Serum" packet down the line of mushers. The train is just departing now . . . the whistle is blowing, I'm waving goodbye to the conductor and away goes the train. What comes next is to bring up the snowmachines, get them into position, and begin to hook up our dog team. Twelve dogs to bootie and twelve dogs to harness. There is a lot of commotion. I've got Chewbacca out here next to the truck. He was just fifty feet away from the train coming in so he got to witness the whole thing."

Minutes later we are given the order to prepare our teams for departure. Each dog team will be assisted by a snowmachine as we depart the train depot and drop down onto the frozen Nenana River. A sturdy cable with quick release hardware is attached between my dog sled and the snowmachine of a team member. The purpose of this tandem setup is to help maintain control of fresh dog teams while we negotiate turns out of town and drop down onto the river. From there, we are on our own.

The dogs, all of them, are screaming to go as I harness and hitch them to the sled. It is my first hookup of all twelve dogs since my last training run in the Washington Cascades. I am struck by the great length of twelve howling dogs stretched out over sixty feet in front of our fragile wooden sled. It is a sobering moment. Minutes later, as several handlers jump in to help guide my dog team through town, we are on our way. We're going to Nome!

We drop down onto the river. It is

Photo credit Evie Wakulenko

" Snow Machine Armada"
Snowmachines hauling cargo sleds loaded with expedition supplies stand ready for departure from the Nenana Railroad Depot

Photo credit Amy Whisler

An Alaskan Railroad official delivers the ceremonial "Serum Package" to expedition trail boss Kent Kantowski

Photo credit Amy Whisler

"The Author"
Von Martin dressed for departure from Nenana

63

"All Lined Out"
Von's Serum Run '25 expedition dog team lined out and ready for departure from Nenana, Alaska
February 22nd, 2009

"Let's Get Moving Already!"
Grits, one of Von's lead dogs, howls to get underway

hard as concrete and within a hundred yards or so, we are on glare ice. The dogs, all twelve, struggle to maintain footholds. Their legs are flailing in different directions as they labor to find traction over the smooth, mirror-like finish. I am reminded of a scene from the movie "Bambi" as the dogs skid and flounder across the ice. How are we ever going to make it all the way to Nome like this? Before us, the quarter mile wide Nenana River stretches out as it weaves a path between rolling, snow laden hills. Yet I can think only of my dogs. I am worried for their safety and quietly wonder, "What have I gotten us into?"

Less than ten miles down river, fate deals another blow from her hidden had of bad fortune. Something is wrong with Blackjack. After leaving the glare ice, the trail becomes drifted over in an even blanket of sugary snow. I am doing the best I can to study Blackjack's gait through forty eight legs as they plow their way down the trail but it is difficult. After hundreds of miles of training, I have made a careful study of every dog's

"Twelve Pack on the Nenana"
Von's team of twelve huskies run on the frozen Nenana River shortly after departure on the first day of the expedition.

movement. When something is wrong, I am quick to notice. While Blackjack remains very hard at work, I can see that one of his back legs isn't "traveling" just right. I immediately stop the team and hook down.

Blackjack is running about midway up the team with Bacon. He studies my approach and looks at me as if to say, "What's up boss?" While he stands there ignoring his condition, I take quick notice that his right rear leg is slightly swollen at the ankle. Blackjack has suffered a serious injury. The dogs are getting anxious to get moving again but I need to help Blackjack and prepare to remove him from the team.

Just then I hear the roar of a snowmachine approaching from behind. I recognize it as one of our expedition machines but can't make out the driver because of their heavy winter gear and helmet. The driver stops just twenty feet away and I motion that I need to give one of my dogs a ride on their sled. Each of the snowmachine cargo trailers include two dog crates provided by the mushers. In the event a dog tires or is injured, these crates can provide them a safe ride to the next checkpoint along the trail. Working quickly, I remove Blackjack from the team and hand him off to the driver of the snowmachine. Meanwhile, my dogs are lunging in their harnesses to get going again and there is no time for a proper goodbye to "Jack". Seconds after handing him off, I pull both hooks and the dogs burst down the trail. Ahead of us, the Nenana River continues its path to the horizon, and threading its frozen course stretches my dog team now numbering eleven.

Photo credit Don Duncan

"Sammys and Sibes"
Veteran Serum Run '25 musher Margaret Black, looks back from her team of Siberian Huskies
while running with veteran musher Don Duncan and his team of Samoyeds on the Nenana River

February 22nd, 2009 - Serum Run Log

"I'm underway on the Nenana River! The time is 2:45 pm. I left with twelve dogs but I had to drop poor Jack as he came up lame very soon into the run. It is his right rear leg I believe. I passed him off to a snow machiner somewhere beyond mile marker ten. The trail is a mixture of extremely glary ice and for the last several miles a very soft, sugary snow - very slow, very hard on the dogs. They're really struggling with this section. But they're just not quitting. Even Teek is moving well. I've got Bacon by himself right smack in the middle of the team. Chewy and Grits have been great up front but we still have a long twelve miles to go. I hope it's not like this all the way to Old Minto."

"3:21 pm and we're still slogging through this sugary trail. Imagine millions and millions of tons of granulated sugar several inches deep. These dogs are just plowing through it. It's really tough going and it's really tough driving the sled . . . my legs are sore and my shoulder hurts. Margaret came up behind me and lost a (sled) runner, and in trying to retrieve it, her team got away from her. Fortu-

nately, as her leaders came up, I caught them and I held them by their neckline."

"Meanwhile, I held my own team with two hooks down. But you hit the river ice several inches below this 'sugary' snow, and you really don't get much grab. Even with both hooks set and my feet on the brake, it's only because (the dogs) know I want them to stop that they're stopping. Rob is up ahead of me. He has had a lot of tangles. Kathy was behind me - lots of tangles with her team. God Bless my dogs. They're not the fastest team down here on the river but I haven't had a tangle yet. They just stay lined out and keep on working. Pike is hanging in there really well and I think he can go all the way if we don't have to go too fast. Teek's struggling in this deep stuff; he doesn't like it a whole lot. Chewy is just unfettered and Grits is right there with him. This is really hard going . . ."

"Sometime just before mile marker twenty, poor Teek finally burned out. He didn't quit running, but he was on his little fanny. So I picked him up and he is laying flat out on top of a very packed sled bag. The team picked up its pace and Pike is trotting along just fine. We're back into some soft stuff again

"Teek Earns a Ride"
Teek rests quietly atop Von's dog sled during the final miles travelled into Old Minto. Teek recovered
quickly after the first day's run and was returned to the team on the second day of the expedition

"Dog Camp at Old Minto"

Huskies from one of the expedition teams rest on straw beds along a cable picket line following the first day's run

but had a nice trail for about a mile. The sun is setting down behind the trees now. We've got about two hours of light remaining and we may or may not make it into Old Minto by dark . . . it's going to depend on this trail and what it gives us."

"5:30 pm - there is a long sunset on my left to the southwest and my dog team has been running non-stop for four and one half hours. Not one stop. They're incredible. I think we may be approaching Old Minto in a bit. We're seeing some buildings for the first time in about thirty miles. We're gonna be ready for a rest. Teek has been a great rider on the way in. The trail has been slow and rough most of the way."

Just as dusk settles over the trail we enter a densely forested area. Minutes later we come upon a dog team camped at the edge of the narrow trail. We have arrived at Old Minto, a small Athebascan village nestled in the woods just off the river. I hook down the team and remove Teek from his balanced perch on the sled bag. Moving quickly through the team, I unclip tuglines from the dog's harnesses and set about removing their booties. This is my signal to them that we are at the end of our run, and they curl

"A Stoic and Heroic Boy"

Backjack rests contently on a bed of straw in Old Minto following his field examination for a serious ankle injury

up into tight circles in the snow while I go about the business of bringing them water, rigging their picket line, and making fresh beds of straw for each. It is a long process, and darkness settles over us long before the last dog is fed and their bowls put away.

While setting up camp, Blackjack is delivered to me and I am very, very happy to see him. I immediately arrange for Dr. Jerry Vanek, one of the expedition's veterinarians, to examine him. Jerry is quick to diagnose Blackjack's injury. He has suffered a "dropped hock", or partial tear of the tendon above his ankle. It is a serious and painful injury and proper treatment will require his leg to be placed into a cast. But doing so in the field will not allow him to fit neatly into a dog crate for transport to a checkpoint where he can be transferred out. In the meantime, Blackjack will have to be carried in a straw filled crate for the next few days. Until his evacuation, we can only offer him medication for his pain and make him as comfortable as possible. It is a grim and sobering finish to our first day's travel on the expedition.

"Dog Camp on Dead Man's Lake"
Von's huskies await hookup from the picket line strung along Dead Man's Lake
prior to their departure from the expedition checkpoint at Beaver Point Lodge
February 24th, 2009

Escape at Dead Man's Lake

"Dogs are miracles with paws"

- Susan Ariel Rainbow Kennedy

February 23rd, 2009 - Serum Run Log

"I left Old Minto at high noon with eleven dogs in the team. It was three miles on a very windy, heavily wooded trail just the width of a dog sled. With trees hanging over about the height of the handlebars, I ducked down for most of the ride. I careened off a few trees pretty hard and ripped the snow hook out of the holster. It just missed my face by an inch . . . but it missed me!"

Photo credit Amy Whisler

"Sled Dog Limousine"
Unable to run another mile, Blackjack gets a ride drawn by Amy Whisler from Old Minto to Beaver Point Lodge, thirty miles distant

"We're crossing a lake. It looks like it's about a mile across. Stretched across the horizon and I can see forests and mountain ranges rising behind them. You can see for miles. There is a blue sky but the sun is very low on the horizon casting long shadows across the snow from the dog team. They are moving along nicely but the trail is sugary and a little slow, so they're working pretty hard."

"It is thirty-five miles to Beaver Point Lodge. We'll see how far Teek can go today, as he is back in harness and moving along! Grits ate breakfast this morning and I was encouraged by that. Taking care of the dogs is really hard when you're parked on a trail ten feet wide, packing water and all your supplies half a mile back and forth in complete darkness between the community house and your dog team."

"The stay at Old Minto was magnificent and the villagers were wonderful. They live in a little village of small, very rustic log cabins. There is no running water. It is taken from the river and heated on a wood fired stove. During the evening, we gathered together in their community house. There were probably twenty-five villagers there and I was being pretty careful to observe their customs. I stayed while they had a "talking circle", and sat quietly observing how they passed the talking stick around, first with the elder, then to

"The Trail of Long Shadows"
The sun, rising just a few degrees above the horizon at mid-day, casts long shadows
from Von's huskies across the trail between Old Minto and Beaver Point Lodge

Dr. Trimble who was talking about health issues. It was then passed to each villager for their chance to talk, one at a time. I was amazed at the respect these people have for their elders, particularly the young people. They were wonderful, hospitable, and soft spoken."

"Best of all, they came out to see the dogs, and a couple of them really took an interest in them. One of the young fellows wanted to know the name of every dog and a little bit about them. The children came out and that was the best part - seeing these native Alaskans come visit these dogs and really take an interest in them. Most of them do not have dogs out here because I don't think they could afford to keep them. I did see a couple of village dogs milling around . . . a couple of oldsters."

"Arrived at Beaver Point Lodge at 5:30 pm. It was a five and a half hour run. Most of this run was through a forest that opened out occasionally onto frozen swamps. We've crossed at least a handful of frozen lakes and some sloughs. The trees are mostly birch and the trail is very windy. Some of it got precarious. I did loose the sled down an embankment and into a ravine that was very deep in snow up

"Alaskan Winter Transportation"
Across the Alaskan interior, the only practical means of winter transportation is by snow machine, airplane, or dog team

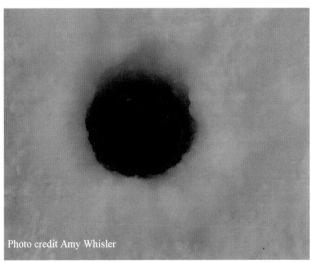

"Alaskan Watering Hole"
A four inch hole drilled through the thick ice above Dead Man's Lake provides water for the teams

to my waist. Fortunately, Mr. Duncan was following behind and came to my rescue. It took the two of us to wrestle my sled plus eleven dogs out of that ravine. I went another hundred yards and across a little wooden bridge before sliding off the crossing and right back down into that ravine. I banged into several trees and lost the snow hook plenty of times."

"But there were some beautiful moments. There was a nice sunny spot in a slough where Don and I stopped and snacked our dogs. I stopped several times to pull booties off of the dogs and put new ones on because they were icing up. I also wanted to check their feet."

"On arrival at Beaver Point Lodge, we parked the teams out on Dead Man's Lake. It is a beautiful vista.

"Flat Out"

Teek (center) lays sprawled out on the ice following a non stop thirty mile run from Old Minto as Pike looks on at right

Teek did the whole run except the last mile around the lake. He was absolutely exhausted. I removed him from the team and he just flopped down flat on top of the dog sled bag! I may give him a rest tomorrow because there will be a fifty mile run out of Manley the next day."

"Blackjack is happy and camped out with his buddy Chewy on Dead Man's Lake. It is extremely remote here. There is a bush plane to get you in and out and that is it. There is no other way unless you've got a dog team."

"It's 9:54 pm and I am standing out-side. It is two degrees above zero and the stars are stunning. I'm looking off to my left and I can see Orion's belt and what appears to be Jupiter above the horizon.

Photo credit Amy Whisler

Steam rising from the cooker condenses in the cold arctic air as Von prepares hot meals for his huskies at the end of a day's run

"Find Your Own Bed"
Blackjack looks over his shoulder from his cozy straw bed

"Arctic Privy With a View"
A single lonely outhouse stands at the edge of the lake

Tonight I jacketed most of the dogs and they're bedded down on cozy beds of straw. I massaged each ankle on most of the dogs and treated their feet with zinc ointment before going in for a bite to eat. I was the last one in for dinner, but the food provided by our hosts was marvelous."

After dinner, everyone is called together for our regular 8:00 pm meeting to discuss the day's run and our plans for tomorrow. I take this opportunity to publicly thank Don Duncan for rescuing me and my dogs out of the ravine we had tumbled into.

Don returns the recognition, with amusement, by thanking me for warning him where all the hazards were on the trail before *he* got to them!

"Who Me?"
Team dog Birch gazes up whimsically with his Disney-like face from his cozy bed and blanket while camped on Dead Man's Lake

Photo credit Amy Whisler

"Musher Accommodations"
A one room cabin provided night-time shelter for at least a dozen members of the expedition team

Don Duncan, musher extraordinaire

Later, after the dogs are bedded down, I prepare to settle in at the cabin for the night. About twelve of us will be camping in the small one room cabin, filled wall to wall with wooden bunks and sleeping bags flopped over portable cots. I am approached by Don Duncan. His face wears a look of concern and I can see there is something troubling him. As he kneels next to me, I see the faint trace of welling in his eyes cast by the yellow light of the small wood stove.

"I'm very sorry to hear about your pup," he says, referring to Black-jack's drop from the team. "You need to know that this expedition is going to include some of the worst experiences of your life, but it will also include some of the *greatest experiences of your life*. It's all part of this journey and you should know that your decision to drop your pup from the team is all a part of this process." His voice lowers as he adds,

"You realize they may not *all* make it to Nome." He studies me with a weak smile, then pats my shoulder and shuffles quietly away. I know exactly what Don is driving at. Anything could happen on any given day to one of these dogs. In spite of our very best care, bad things sometimes happen. Last night things had ended with the heartbreaking news of Blackjack's injury and loss from our team. Tonight was ending with the equally sobering thought that it could happen again. There were still hundreds of miles of Alaskan wilderness to cover. And the worst was still to come.

Making myself as comfortable as possible on a portable cot, I slip, fully dressed into my sleeping bag for the night. As the temperature outside tumbles to well below zero, I am comforted with the thought that, for the time, my dogs are safely picketed only a hundred yards away. But I couldn't have been more wrong. Even as I drift off to sleep, fate is already at work with her next plot of misfortune. Down on the lake, Pike is moving around on his line. Somehow in his restlessness, perhaps because he is bored, or maybe just nervous about being picketed on a lake hundreds of miles from nowhere, he manages to escape.

In his restless pacing about, one of the heavy bronze snaps securing him to the cable picket line becomes snagged and suddenly pops loose. Pike is free on the lake. In near total darkness, he moves at liberty about the dog lot, lit only by stars that stretch from horizon to horizon. Guided by his keen sense of smell, he is drawn to the spot where I had prepared their meals and grazes there for a time, scavenging for snacks. Wandering stealthily away from his team mates, there is nothing at all to stop him from crossing the lake, drifting down a lonely trail, and becoming part of the Alaskan wilderness.

"Dawn Over Dead Man's Lake"
Expedition team mushers and their snowmachine partners prepare dogs and gear for another day on the trail

"Snack Time On the River"
Lead dogs Grits (L) and Chewbacca (R), await their mid day serving of frozen meat snacks
while Tigger (center) and the rest of the team looks on

Blackjack's Farewell

"A man and his dog are a sacred relationship"

- A.R. Gurney

Photo credit Amy Whisler

"Back In My Arms"
A "breathcicle" dangles from Von's face in subzero temps as he embraces Pike's return following his escape

February 24th, 2009 - Serum Run Log

"Pike got loose last night. This morning he was found out on the lake wandering around the camp. He was spotted peeing on Margaret's sled and she was able to grab him and put him back on the picket line! He still had his neckline portion on."

"9:43 am - we arose this morning at 6:00 am while the temperature was still eight degrees below zero. I looked after the dogs before coming down for breakfast and our typical morning meeting. The run today will be from Beaver Point Lodge to Manley Hot Springs. The distance is approximately thirty-five miles. It will begin by crossing Dead Man's Lake about a mile or two across before entering the woods. The trail will move through typical northern Alaska flat lands, rolling terrain, spruce forests, across open sloughs, frozen lakes, and along rivers."

"The dogs are looking good. I may give Teek a ride to today - as the next leg is a long run leaving Manley. Most of the dogs were jacketed last night and they seemed to enjoy that. Grits ate well this morning; four pieces of lamb and most of a can of food, so his appetite is picking up a bit. At this time, I am about to bootie dogs and we will be moving sometime after 10:30 am. That gives me forty-five minutes to bootie and harness dogs, roll up the lines, and head out across this lake on another day of adventure."

"The time is 1:00 pm. We got underway from Beaver Point Lodge at approximately 11:35 am. This will be a short entry because I'm barehanded here. It's pretty cold and I'm trying to hold onto my voice recorder and drive with the other hand. We passed the ten mile marker one hour and twenty minutes into the run. We're now passing through mostly tundra mixed with black spruce forests. The dogs are doing well."

"Rise and Shine"
Musher, Don Duncan, rallies one of his "kids" as he
prepared to dress and bootie his team of Samoyeds

"We passed the twenty mile marker at 2:23 pm. The trail continues to be a mixture of lake crossings, slough crossings, marsh crossings, and forests dominated by black spruce and some birch. The skies are still partly cloudy and I don't have a thermometer but it feels pretty close to zero today. I'm really keeping an eye on Pike. He seems a little more tired than he has been but he's still trotting along. I stopped to change booties on him but his stride is not looking as easy today. Saw some moose tracks but didn't see the critter - thank goodness."

"I'm doing a lot of this run with Duncan today. I passed him back on a slough and he is back behind me there a bit. We're kinda running together today. We've got about fourteen miles to go on this run. I'm passing some of the old telegraph line on the way and seeing some of the wire. It's just five or six feet above the trail here!"

After running about four and a half hours while navigating a narrow trail through the woods, I hear a snowmachine approach from the behind. I can see it is one of our expedition machiners. I stop my dogs and usher them to the side of the trail. The snow-

"Hike!"
Von's dog team gets underway while crossing Dead Man's Lake near Beaver Point Lodge.
L to R are Pike, Willow, Bacon, Cherry, Birch, and Tigger. Out of view are Patrick, Boomer, Chewy and Grits

Photo credit Evie Wakulenko

"Cheshire Husky"
Teek grins from ear to ear during his ride to Manley Hot Springs drawn by medical team specialist, Evie Wakulenko. Teek was offered a day of rest to prepare for the long sixty miles run to Tanana
February 25, 2009

machine is hauling a sled with a dog crate strapped on the back. I'm standing up front holding my lead dogs to the side so the machiner can pass safely on the narrow trail.

As the sled bearing the dog crate passes by, my attention is drawn to a 'Cheshire Grin' painted across the face of a husky riding inside. It's Teek! He is looking out the back door with a silly grin on his face that seems to be saying, "Hey, look at me! Now this is what I call mushing!"

He really looks like he is enjoying himself. He studies all the dogs as he glides easily by and they can see him too. Then off he goes, as the machine picks up speed and pulls away. I can still make out the 'Cheshire Grin' plastered over his face as he fades into the distance until I finally lose sight of him about a quarter of a mile up the trail.

"Passing through more birch and spruce. It's just a long and winding trail through the woods hour after hour. I hope to be in before sunset and to be taking care of the dogs. Everyday we leave later and the run is longer, so we're out later every day."

February 25th, 2009 - Serum Run Log

"It is 2:30 pm in Manley, Alaska. There is a slight breeze. The temperature is twenty degrees and the skies are mostly cloudy. I am sitting in the dog lot with my dogs and I'm the only musher out here. I've just finished "souping" and "snacking" the dogs, and scooping up after them. I'm walking up and down the line and petting everybody while talking to them."

"We've had a really great experience here in Manley and the folks are wonderful. We are staying in a school with a student population of ten. The children range in age from about third or fourth grade right up to senior high. They have hot and cold running water and bathrooms but they don't work. There are two outhouses constructed of plywood situated outside the school building for us to use. A well used piece of Styrofoam with a hole in it, is provided to keep you off of the plywood seat when it is

"Trail on the Slough"

"The trail to Manley continues to be a mixture of lake crossings, slough crossings, marsh crossings, and forests dominated by black spruce and some birch" - Serum Run Log

fifty or sixty below zero."

"The dogs are on rest day today. Soon I'm going to pack the sled for tomorrow's nearly sixty mile run. We will climb a mountain range and then pass through a mining camp. After thirty or forty miles, we'll cross Fish Lake that is four miles across. Then we will hit the Haystack Slough, which is supposed to be pretty treacherous prior to our arrival in Tanana. This will be the biggest test for these dogs. I'm told by Don and Margaret that it will sort out who's going to Nome or not, so I'll have my eyes on my Sibes."

"The dogs are enjoying their blankets. I have a picket line stretching in front of me probably a hundred and fifty feet long with the dogs spaced out along it. They've got their straw and their dog blankets and they're eating and drinking better everyday and getting a little more accustomed to trail life. They are separated from the other dogs teams by three to ten feet so they are also getting accustomed to eating and sleeping with other teams around them."

"It's hard to explain every detail about being here. Being with the local people, experiencing this incredible journey, and knowing that every mile traveled has been by these dogs. It's an unbelievable experience . . . not like taking a bus, or a train, or a plane, or even riding your bike somewhere. It's what you are seeing as they take you over sloughs, up berms and onto trails and - Oh God - it is exhilarating. And sometimes it is terrifying."

"Into the Woods"
With Chewbacca and Grits leading the way, Von's team climbs off a river and enters a forest of
mixed birch and spruce. Along the way, vestiges of the original telegraph line that carried
messages calling dog teams to action in 1925 can still be seen near the edge of the trail

"Can We Take Him Home?"
Blackjack is delivered to Von's dog camp at Manley Hot Springs by expedition team veterinarian
Lyndall Soule (left) and medical team specialist Amy Whisler (right). After four long days carried on the trail,
"Jack" was able to be shipped to a Fairbanks animal hospital where he received complete medical care.

Today I sent Blackjack off to Fairbanks. He made no objection when I lifted him into the little box that would be his ride up to a Fairbanks animal hospital. He was my second casualty since preparing for the expedition, and another fine husky that would never see the beaches of Nome. As I kissed his muzzle farewell, I could still recall the cheerfulness of his wide smile at our first meeting in Spokane, of our long ride home on that hot summer day, and even of the skunk fumes we endured along the way. "How could this have happened to my youngest and sturdiest dog?" I wondered. Then I gave "Jack" one last stroke of affection and sent him on his way.

I'm wearing my thickest skin as I walk from my little black and white canine buddy. I had never really thought about all of us not being together at the end in Nome. Somehow I had imagined all of us arriving there together. It was hard to accept the fate that had been dealt ole "Jack". Still, when I gazed into his eyes and bid him adieu, I made the best effort I could to convince him that everything is going

"Layover at Manley Hot Springs"
Due to delays required for numerous snowmachine repairs, the dog teams were able to enjoy an extra day's rest while camped in the snowfield near Manley
February 25, 2009

to be just fine. Now I just need to convince *myself*. It takes all the strength I have to separate myself from him, and it's not like any hardship I've had to endure so far.

Even so, I need to give all my attention to these guys that are still here with me. I've got to rouse them up and be cheerful with them. You can never look like you're down because they'll pick it right up, and they'll sense it from you *immediately*.

Every time I walk by them, I'm reaching down with my hand, caressing their ears, and saying their name. I'm giving them happy talk and singing them songs. Mostly I am telling them, "This is exciting, and I can't wait to have another day with you on the trail." It is a big part of running dogs. They need to know that I'm okay, so they can feel okay.

"6:45 pm - I've just fed the dogs as much food as I can get them to take before our very long run tomorrow - perhaps our longest run of the Serum Run. I'm a little worried about this run, particularly for Pike and Teek. If they both get too tired, I can't carry them both so I'll need some help with at least one of them. This is the run that will make or break each dog and decides who continues on."

"Today I gave each of them all the hydration that I could. In the morning I'm going to feed the dogs a breakfast of lamb soaked in water, a little kibble, and some Impact. Right now they're still jacketed and nested down. They've had a balmy rest today with no wind, so hopefully they're all raring to go in the morning. For most, it's going to be the longest run of their careers."

"We're expecting some overflow tomorrow, so I'll have my extra pair of boots onboard. I am told we may see some wind tomorrow in the hills. I wish my dogs God Speed."

Photo credit Don Duncan

"Sleepy Girl"
One of Don Duncan's Samoyed sled dogs slumbers in the late afternoon sun in Manley Hot Springs after finishing her bowl of food

"Ground Blizzard"

Von's team of eleven remaining huskies heroically battle 50+ mph headwinds as they emerge from
a ground blizzard while carrying the "Serum" on a frozen lake crossing in sub zero temperatures.
The fifty-seven mile run from Manley to Tanana was the single longest leg of the Serum Run Expedition

Serum Delivery to Tanana

"Please engage your dog teams to carry antitoxin to Tanana"

- Alaska Governor Scott C. Bone - January 26, 1925

"Playtime For Teek"
Teek romps in deep snow following his arrival into Manley
as medical team specialist, Evie Wakulenko, RN looks on

Due to numerous snowmachine mechanical failures, we are forced to spend an extra night in Manley which puts the team one day behind schedule. But at this point we don't plan to do double miles per day to make up the time.

Almost from the start of the expedition, our snowmachine team is plagued with bad fortune. On the trail from Old Minto, the engine of one machine froze up which caused it to be stuck out on the trail. The snowmachine had to be towed into Manley and a replacement machine purchased. There are countless snags with trees and brush, and numerous sled loads were toppled after becoming unstable while traversing rough sections of trail.

While in Manley, the transmission on Dr. Vanek's snowmachine failed and by the time parts are delivered in, they are up all night trying to repair it.

On the 26th, the ongoing saga of bad weather reported for the coast now appears to threaten the Alaskan interior. In the early morning hours of February 26th, a snowmachine team member observes, "We're also hearing about the blizzard further out west that dumped at least 4 more feet of snow on some areas (that) we need to cross - heard some folks tried to get to Nome on snowmachines and had to turn back. Guess we'll deal with that next . . ."

February 26th, 2009 - Serum Run Log

"8:12 am - light snow flurries - temperature approximately 10 degrees. Today my dogs and I are carrying the Serum from Manley to Tanana! The dogs all look good this morning - everyone ate

"Spills and Thrills"
Evie Wakulenko, (L) and MaryLou Fram (center)
rush to assist team veterinarian Lyndall Soule (R),
after her snowmachine flounders in soft snow

breakfast. *Even Teek had something. Not sure how far he'll make it. I'll see if I can get thirty miles out of him and forty-five out of Pike. I think all the others can do sixty miles. Their blankets are off and packed. I'm ready to rake straw and then start powdering and putting their booties on."*

"I have departed Manley. The time is 10:37 am and it is snowing moderately. Got underway with a little mayhem. 11:55 am - we've just passed the ten mile marker. 1:35 pm - we're now passing the twenty mile marker while working our way through a moderately dense forest of small black spruce. The terrain is slightly rolling and we are receiving moderate snowfall under cloudy skies. There is a brisk breeze coming right at us so it's a little cool. The trail here is punchy in sections, and just slow. We are moving along at about six or seven miles an hour tops. But it's a steady pace and the dogs are working pretty hard. I've put some drag on the track to slow the mutts down a bit. It's a little bumpy . . . and a lot of moguls. We lost our nice hard packed trail."

"Looking off to the horizon on my right, there are hills, rolling and forested, rising up . . . I'd say upwards to a thousand or fifteen hundred feet. We passed a couple of quail coming out of their little burrow to watch our dog team come by. Some ravens also came by to observe us. I not real sure we're on the right section of trail here - it split off. Okay . . . now I see dog urine on the way ahead so we must be on the right trail!"

Later in the day, we experience a close scrape that nearly spells the end of our run to Nome. About 3:00 pm our team is approached from behind by a snowmachine ridden by Dr. Jerry Vanek, one of our team veterinarians. The trail is narrow with deep, soft shoulders flanking each side that will make overtaking my team hazardous. Eventually, we approach a stretch that seems to hold promise for a safe pass. By mutual agreement, Jerry and I decided this is a good

"Bridge Crossing Out of Manley"
Von and his eleven huskies are helped out of Manley by a snowmachine in route to Tanana fifty-seven miles distant

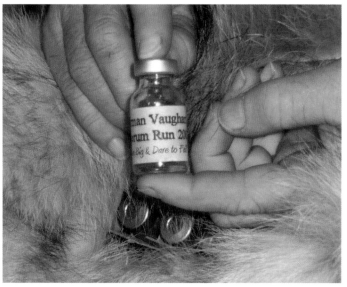

"The Serum"
The ceremonial " Serum" is carefully insulated and packed to guard against freezing during the expedition

"Precious Cargo"
Von's dog team enters the Tofti Hills under moderate snowfall while carrying the ceremonial
"Serum" from Manley Hot Springs to Tanana, fifty-seven miles distant on the Yukon River

place for him to pass us and I call my team to a halt. Jerry's snowmachine is towing heavy cargo and as he edges carefully past my sled, then drawing even with the dogs, his snowmachine suddenly flounders in soft snow and begins an unstoppable, slow motion roll to the left - directly into my dog team!

Watching in horror, I stand nearly paralyzed on my sled runners as his snowmachine rolls nearly 180 degrees directly into the team where Pike and Teek cower helplessly tethered to the gangling. It all happens so quickly that there is no chance to save my dogs. In seconds the machine is nearly upside down with Jerry, unharmed, partially buried underneath. Miraculously, Pike and Teek avoid injury by crabbing to the left, leaving just inches between them and the inverted snowmachine. Fortunately for man and dogs, no one is hurt.

Springing into action, I hook down the team and run forward to help Jerry to his feet. But all he wants to know is how the dogs are doing. Laughing almost hysterically, I tell him, "It's okay Jerry, they're fine. My dogs crowded to the left and your machine missed them by eighteen inches!" After wrestling with his snowmachine, Jerry and I somehow manage to get it righted while Pike, Teek, and all the huskies watch nervously with lowered heads. In minutes, Jerry has his machine restarted, and with a wave, continues safely past Chewy and Grits and down the trail. I almost have to chuckle at the irony of our close call - my dog team nearly taken out by the expedition's veterinarian! Jerry later felt apologetic about the incident but it really wasn't his fault as neither of us foresaw the danger. It was definitely a heart stopping interlude to our long day's run and we still have thirty miles to go into Tanana!

"The Great Alaskan Interior"
*"There are few lonely places in this world, and the wastes of the great
Alaskan Interior are the loneliest of them all . . ."* - Henry W. Elliott

"Everybody Okay?"
Von prepares to change booties on his huskies following white-out
conditions during a frozen lake crossing on the trail to Tanana

About 25 miles out on the trail, several of the snowmachines become bogged down at a perilous ravine crossing known as American Creek. After dropping off a steep hill, the trail crosses a frozen creek before rising sharply uphill. Near the top of the hill, the trail hooks hazardously to the left around a big tree. It is here that just about every snowmachiner gets caught up.

Some of the drivers attempt to make the crossing by 'jamming' their machines across the creek only to bog out on the turn. One machine fries a drive belt. Another machine and cargo sled become stuck and can't be moved. Just as the other machiners stop to help, the dog teams start rolling up on their tails and things turn into a real mess.

Fortunately, with the help of several dismounted snowmachiners, the trail is yielded to our dog teams who, one by one, manage to negotiate safely through the obstacles of stalled machines, cargo sleds, bad trail, and trees.

"At 3:55 pm, we passed the thirty mile marker. Most of the snowmachiners were there as we entered a very deep ravine with a sharp turn going into it with some ice and overflow. After climbing an extremely steep hill, I flipped my sled on its side and ran the runners around a big tree blocking our way."

But the worst of the day's run is still ahead. Late in the afternoon, we are overtaken by a ground blizzard during the crossing of a large frozen lake. Later I will learn that people have become lost during its traverse because there are multiple tracks crossing it and you can barely see from one side to the other, particularly during the white out conditions we experienced.

"Frozen Face, Warm Heart"
Pike reclines with his face encrusted in ice shortly after encountering a ground blizzard while crossing Fish Lake

"We've been crossing an open landscape for some miles now . . . we came out of the woods and dropped down onto . . . I wasn't sure if it was a river or a lake but it was vast as far as the eye could see. It was solid white and there was a ground blizzard blowing across it. We dropped down onto it and we were right into the wind. I know we are having at least 50 mph sustained winds and drifting snow - the trail is completely obliterated and I can see nothing - it looks just like the moon. But by golly, these dogs just started out across it."

"There is no visible trail but there is probably a 'scent trail' over the ice, and Chewy and Grits are carrying us across. Tripod markers set up by the State of Alaska are helping to mark the way. The dogs are absolutely incredible . . . their faces are just frozen. I have my hood pulled completely over my face so I can barely see but the dogs have not stopped. They are frosted all the way up to their thighs and their faces are solid white. We are in a complete white-out and visibility is close to zero. It's a rather frightful crossing of this ice - a frozen lake perhaps. This might be Fish Lake. I can't see the shore behind me. It's completely obliterated by the blizzard but I can just make out a shoreline ahead. Now and then Chewbacca turns to look at me. I know he just wants to make sure everything is okay with me because everything is still okay with him. Hopefully, in another half an hour we're out of this. The wind is just howling."

In a feeble attempt to dodge the biting wind, I duck behind my dogsled. But there is little escape from gale force winds roaring in my ears and clawing at my skin. Rattling in the wind just inches from my face are Wolfie's old dog tags and her collar that I had attached to the driving bow. I'm remember-

"Team Work"
Expedition team members load Teek into a crate drawn by a snowmachine shortly after emerging from a ground blizzard

ing back to the day I put her down, and of the promise I made about going to Nome together by dog team. Above the nostalgic 'jingling' of her old metal dog tags I cry out, *"Wolfie . . . just what have we gotten ourselves into?"*

Arriving at the far side of the lake, we pick up the trail where it enters a lightly wooded area before opening out into another lake. We are safely out of the blizzard. I hook down my team as all the dogs shake most of the ice from their coats. Marching steadily to the front of the team, I stop to pet and thank each dog for their hard work. They are all eager to continue, except for little Teek who has finally grown weary. As I prepare to offer him a ride atop the dogsled, Dr. Trimble arrives on his snowmachine and offers to carry Teek aboard his cargo sled for the rest of the journey into Tanana. After securing Teek in a cozy crate aboard the cargo sled and replacing several frozen booties on the dogs, we are back on our way.

"9:30 pm - my dogs have been running for eleven hours nonstop - we're delivering the Serum to Tanana. I dropped Teek from the team at mile thirty-five, and still have ten dogs in harness. Just min-

utes ago we dropped down onto the Yukon River after running for three hours in the pitch dark. We've got clear skies and no moon and I'm picking out an airport beacon up ahead . . . I can't tell the range but I know we're on the Yukon. We dropped down onto it from a very steep embankment and really hit the ice hard. Patrick fell and got dragged a bit but I think he's okay. We've got Venus right up in front

"Glowing Eyes"
Warm meals are prepared for Von's huskies at their dog camp in Tanana as the dogs look on with glowing eyes

of us about seven degrees above the horizon and we're aiming right at her. I really hope we get into Tanana soon. It's terribly cold and the dogs all have several inches of ice hanging from their faces. Some of them are coming up a little sore. But Pike is still running!"

"The time is 10:05 pm. We are off the Yukon River and the dogs are moving along at a very fast trot . . . we're less an a half mile, I understand, from our destination. So it's been a very long day. We have a beautiful clear starry night. Very dark out - very spectacular - and very cold."

In fact, the temperature has dropped to 12 degrees below zero. Minutes later my team approaches a large log structure partially obscured in the inky black of night near the edge of the Yukon River. It is the old Tanana Road House. I am directed into to a parking area flanked by brush and small trees. Calling the dogs to a halt, I hit the brake and hook down the sled. After running non-stop for eleven and a half hours, we have safely delivered the Serum to Tanana. My first sense of duty is to look after my dogs. Then removing the insulated Serum package from my sled bag, I enter the old road house and present it to our expedition team coordinator, Erin McLarnon.

"The Road House at Tanana"
Von's dogs sleep through the day in deep snow at their camp just out side the Tanana Road House
following one of several heavy snowstorms that swept down the Yukon River into Tanana

February 27th, 2009

By dawn, the temperature has dropped to 34 degrees below zero. Today we receive word from Phil Pryzmont, our missing snowmachiner, who was found on the Kaltage portage a few days back. He is stranded with a broken snowmachine and awaiting parts to be delivered by air. At 6:36 pm he forwards a gloomy communication to our team. *"My parts aren't here yet; we're having a helluva storm on the coast. I don't know yet when I'll meet up with you."*

While we are relieved to know Phil is well, his report is a dire forecast of weather awaiting the rest of our team. At 7:11 pm, our expedition team leaders are sent a second ominous weather report. *"Alaska weather is about to get interesting . . . a blowing 50+ mph winds winter storm is coming into west coast tonight, Friday . . . predictions are to roll across Alaska this weekend."*

"9:19 pm - the temperature is close to zero. It is snowing heavily and winds are now gusting 25 to

30 mph. I've tucked all the dogs in and they're getting deeply covered in snow. It's a very dry snow and hopefully it has an insulating factor for them. They all have jackets on and I've refreshed their straw. I offered them a heavy feeding this evening, so that makes three feedings for today."

"The dogs are looking pretty fit. I'm giving Teek a ride tomorrow for the sixty mile run, so I've switched the gang line set up for ten dogs. I'll put Pike in the team ahead of Boomer and Patrick where he can run with Bacon who will perform very well that day. I'm putting Birch and Willow back in the mid team section, the girls up in swing position, and Chewy and Grits in lead. If there is any trouble up front, I'll give Willow a shot at it but I don't want to take lead away from Chewy right now. He's been performing real well and I want him to own that role as long as he can. Today I learned that Jack is doing well in Fairbanks and did not require surgery! He is in a leg cast due to a partial tear of the Achilles tendon. We are hopeful for a full recovery and his return to service next season."

In a message relayed from Fairbanks to the expedition team, Greg Newby reports, "Blackjack now has a walking cast and will keep it for 2-3 weeks. He is resting comfortably, and getting along superbly with our other dogs. It's a good test of a dog's temperament to bring him into a yard where 9 other dogs are running loose! He's probably not quite sure where he is, but doesn't seem to be taking things badly."

Serum Run Log (continued)

"Our team is being warned about a moose sighting approximately forty miles out on the trail. There is a calf stuck in the snow and a cow hanging around. There was much discussion about how to best handle this dangerous obstacle. While the river is a mile wide, the trail is only the width of a snow-machine and a moose is not likely to yield the trail. Don and Margaret are packing flare guns. When I come up on the moose, unless it's snowing heavily, I should be able to spot it at least half a mile out. Then I'm going to hook down the team and wait for a snowmachiner to come up. I'm told that moose will often run from a snowmachine if the driver dismounts and runs toward them. They mistake them for hunters and run off. On the other hand, a moose will mistake dog teams for wolves, and will attack them. So we are at a disadvantage in that regard."

"Tomorrow morning we plan to 'pull hook' at 9:30 am and get down to the Yukon where the village elders can witness our departure. Then it will be sixty miles down the Yukon River to the vicinity of Nine Mile Cabin for a camp-out with the team. From there we'll resume on February 29th for a sixty mile run to Ruby. The trail was set today by local villages running from Ruby towards us and from here back their way. It's now open but we're having a pretty good snowstorm roll in. We'll see what we get storm wise. This could get very interesting . . ."

"Delay at Tanana"
Von and his remaining eleven huskies wait at their dog camp
in Tanana for trail conditions to improve on the Yukon River

"Sled Dog Shuttle Service"
Von and his huskies speed down the trail in a plywood 'boxcar' drawn by a snowmachine in route to the Tanana airstrip.
Delays due to snowstorms required the dog teams to be air portaged over a hazardous length of the Yukon River

When Huskies Fly

*"One of the most enduring friendships in history -
dogs and their people, people and their dogs"*

- Terry Kay

February 28th, 2009 - Serum Run Log

"We had a pretty good dump of snow last night and winds gusting to 35 mph. The dogs were in their jackets last night. This morning they all got ear rubs and everybody is standing with wagging tails today. Hopefully, that frontal system has moved through and we won't encounter anymore snowfall. What we really don't want are winds that could drift the snow back across the trail. We are hoping to leave about 9:30 am and expect a long run of ten hours or more. It all depends on what the weather brings us. What a difference a few hours can make here on the Yukon."

"When Hell Freezes Over"
The mighty Yukon River lies buried under a hazardous deluge of snow after a coastal storm moved into the Alaskan interior on February 27th. Up to six feet of fresh snow rendered travel on the Yukon nearly impossible

"It is 10:16 am - an extraordinary set of circumstances has called for an extraordinary decision. We've just come from an hour long meeting with our expedition team to address the issue of extreme weather and current trail conditions on the Yukon between Tanana and Ruby. Last night's storm sys-

tem pretty much obliterated our trail. It might still be possible to travel on it but it would require three days and two nights to get to Ruby and we are short of food between here and there."

"We have hurricane force winds on the coast bringing in more weather. We have another storm headed our way and more snow anticipated for the next several days over the Yukon. If we encounter more severe weather on the coast - and we are looking at that as a very real possibility, we could find ourselves arriving in Nome at a time when we might be stranded for weeks and unable to get out on air cargo due to Iditarod."

"We were faced with a very hard decision and there was a lot of discussion around our group of mushers. The general consensus is that while we are disappointed we won't be running this section of the Yukon, we want to make sure our dogs are safe and that they get into Galena with wagging tails and the surpluses of food that they are going to need. So we are talking about 'air portaging' our dogs one hundred and twenty miles to Ruby. My vote is to fly as little as we have to and to make the run from Ruby to Galena. It is fairly well traveled by the villagers and we should be able to get through there okay."

"We've made the decision to fly to Ruby, and Erin is communicating with an air cargo service. This is going to be a little like those Antarctic expeditions where the huskies are placed on picket lines down the length of a cargo plane. The dogs will be picketed by chains to the bulkhead . . . and dogsleds put onboard fully loaded with every bit of supplies you're going to need for you and your dogs for at least

"Stormy Weather"
Von and some of his huskies await the arrival of their single engine Cessna for 'air portage' over an impassable section of the Yukon River to Ruby.   Pictured L to R are Patrick, Boomer, Birch. Grits, and Willow

"Ready to Fly"
Siberian Huskies Teek (foreground) and Pike (standing) wait with Von's dogs for the arrival of a single engine Cessna to carry them to Ruby, one hundred and twenty miles down the Yukon River

twenty-four hours. It's going to take several shuttle runs by cargo planes to get all the teams moved. If we can get all the sleds and the teams out today, we will do so. If not, it'll spill over into tomorrow."

"Meanwhile, the snowmachines will attempt to punch through one hundred and twenty miles to Ruby and they've got the fuel to do that. The dog teams could do it but there is a problem with food shortages due to the fact we're already behind schedule. I am about to go through my sled and make sure I have everything I need for twenty-four hours of running, camping, and caring for my dogs. I'm going to put harnesses and dog blankets in for the dogs, I'm carrying my cooker, all the dog bowls, one gallon of Heet, food and snacks for myself and the dogs, my sleeping bag, and

"Tanana Departure"
Musher Don Duncan prepares his team of twelve Samoyeds for 'air portage' to Ruby aboard a single engine Cessna Caravan. Each airplane relay included two expedition dogsleds, twenty four huskies, and their drivers

"When Huskies Fly"

Expedition team leader, Erin McLarnon (left) prepares to receive Birch, one of Von's team dogs from medical team specialist, Evie Wakulenko (right) aboard a chartered single engine Cessna

of course the picket lines."

"I want to look at this situation as an extraordinary opportunity. I told some of my team members that this will be the year they look back on and recall, 'Remember what happened back in '09 when we portaged all those dogs over the Yukon?' One of the things that separates an expedition from a vacation is the unknown. Sometimes that unknown changes not just day to day but from hour to hour. It's driven by weather, logistics, unforeseeable conditions, and decisions by team members acting as a cohesive unit because we're not a bunch of individuals out on vacation. We are here on this expedition to take whatever comes our way. And what we're learning most of the time is, things happen quite unexpectedly and you're working with circumstances that are new each day. It's about being innovative, accepting what comes, doing the best you can, and letting that be the legacy of this adventure."

There is a small airstrip about a mile outside of Tanana where our dogs, sleds, and gear will be loaded onto small planes and flown to Ruby. Half the fun is just getting to the airstrip. The huskies must be tightly packed, a team at a time, into an open top plywood box with runners, then towed by snowmachine to the airstrip. Most of the dogs are pretty anxious about this and somehow sense they'll be missing another day out on the trail.

First I lift Chewbacca into the box measuring barely two feet across by eight feet in length. Then one by one, I place my other ten huskies into the box, where they are restrained from leaping out by a very short chain. This is stressful to some of the dogs, and a few begin to cry. After the dogs are loaded, we are hitched to a snowmachine while my dogsled will skid along behind from a short tow rope. Our ride to the airstrip is mostly uneventful until our last turn. Without warning, the coupler joining our plywood 'boxcar' to the snowmachine comes unhitched, and we are flung out of control like a wild coal car ride from an Indian Jones film. Riding on top of the box, I have absolutely no way to stop or steer, and all I can do is wait for our careening ride to come to a coasting stop.

Shortly, the snowmachine returns for us, and we are towed to an open, vacant area. Seeing no airplanes, buildings, or structures of any kind I ask if this is the airstrip. Someone points to a lonely orange windsock blowing from a masthead. Apparently we're *standing* on the airstrip. In a few minutes a second snowmachine arrives towing the team of musher, Alana Kingsley, and all her gear. Somehow we will be expected to load nearly twenty-four huskies, two fully packed expedition sleds, and ourselves onto a small aircraft. The question is, how small?

In a few minutes, a single engine Cessna appears from the snowstorm at the edge of the airstrip. It is terribly small, and I'm wondering how we're ever going to manage to get everything safely on board. After landing, a small door at the side of the Cessna is opened and we waste no time loading gear and dogs. Another wind driven snowstorm is about to bear down on us. First we load Alana's twelve huskies, shoulder to shoulder, along the length of the stubby cargo area. Each husky is secured by a neckline to a cable running the length of the aircraft. Next we load the two heavily packed dogsleds. It's a tight fit, and we are forced to stack my sled upside down on top of Alana's. This requires the removal of nearly all my carefully packed contents, including Wolfie's little tin of ashes, that are tossed, ramshackle, into a small bay in the belly of the plane.

After wrestling my sled into the airplane, there seems little room for anything else, let alone my entire dog team. As strong winds driving a wall of white weather approaches the little Cessna, we quickly load

"Preflight Jitters"
Von's lead dog, Chewbacca, peers wistfully at him from the back of the plane just prior to take-off during a blizzard in Tanana

all eleven of my huskies, practically one atop the other into the little remaining space. Teek is the last husky to be loaded, and as I prepare to stuff him into the last few square inches, the blizzard descends upon us. Teek has always had a special affection for the movie 'Eight Below', about the dogs stranded in an Antarctic storm, and has sat through the DVD several times. Just prior to the cargo hatch being closed for our departure, I give Teek a final hug and tell him, "Well Teek, you've always loved the movie 'Eight Below' . . . well, now you're *in* the movie!"

Our pilot slams the hatch closed with a clank and I can see Teek and the dogs looking wistfully out the tiny window. The wind gains strength and snow is blowing sidewise down the length of the fragile looking Cessna. Turning to the pilot, I ask, "Are we okay in all this?" His reply is brief and to the point. Redirecting my attention to the flimsy passenger door he says flatly, "Get in."

"The time is 3:21 pm. Musher Alana Kingsley and I have all our dogs on board a small Cessna . . . by my count twenty-three huskies on board a single engine aircraft with our two dogsleds in the middle of the cargo area! The dogs are necklined to a cable around the bulkhead. They are shoulder to shoul-

"A Full Flight"
The view from Von's jump seat showing crowded conditions aboard their chartered single engine Cessna with twenty-three sled dogs picketed to the airplane's bulkheads and two expedition dogsleds stacked one atop the other

der; literary on top of each other. Chewy is looking out the window but he can't see because we're essentially taking off in a blizzard. Teek looks a little stressed, he's panting . . . his head is shaking and he's in the very back next to 'Pikey Boy'. He has the emergency exit door to work. The dogs are being good dogs and Chewy is being a good boy. He's over there by Willow and he's got little Tigger next to him, and Grits on the other side. Patrick and Boomer are kinda stuffed in the back. In fact, Boomer's got his head on Teek's back. And Cherry's up here next to Alana's dogs. I'm in the jump seat, where I'm going to be keeping an eye on these dogs and looking for shifting cargo."

It is nothing short of amazing that my huskies, some of whom might otherwise fight with a neighbor in such close quarters, have struck a kind of temporary, unspoken truce while frightfully crammed like sardines into the vibrating Cessna. I can see little out the windshield beyond the propeller's blur as the pilot revs the engine and we are propelled forward through a wall of white. The dogs immediately drop down, cowering one upon the other with ears flattened and heads trembling. Our big brave huskies are reduced to shuddering bags of jelly as the Cessna rolls over the snowfield and is carried into the air. All except for Chewbacca. With flattened ears he peers just over the edge of the window. "Don't worry kids", I shout to them. "Whatever happens next, at least we're all in this together!" In spite of my effort to console their fear, most of the dogs make the bouncy, forty minute flight with bowed heads and quivering ears.

"We're in route to Ruby and the dogs are doing okay. Chewy is looking out the window when he can. His eyes are the size of saucers with an expression that seems to say, 'What are we doing way up here?' We're flying along at about 1,300 feet, so we're getting a good view of the Yukon down there and Alaska in midwinter. Chewy is starting to settle down a bit now. His ears are back and he is just looking out the window and watching the scenery go by. He's the only one looking out the window, everyone else has got their heads down . . ."

Back in Tanana, our team of eleven snowmachiners are organizing their caravan of machines and cargo sleds as they prepare to make their departure. The day before, a local snowmachiner had been hired to break trail to Ruby. However, by early morning the trail is blown over due to the blizzard, which continues off and on throughout the day. In spite of the dismal conditions, our cargo train of

Photo credit: Amy Whisler

"Trail of Broken Dreams"
Members of the expedition's snowmachine party watch as an approaching blizzard bears down on them while their machines and cargo flounder in a "bottomless" trail along the Yukon River near Tanana

103

twelve snowmachines and their riders descend the steep banks of the Yukon River and led by Paul, a local village guide, begins its westward crawl towards Ruby. Struggling against four to six feet of soft snow, the snowmachiners spend a grueling day in a hopeless attempt to break new trail.

About ten miles out, Paul who is running ahead of team, suddenly faces a rapidly approaching blizzard. Turning around and racing back to the expedition team, he orders "Drop your sleds, turn and go! There's a wall of white coming towards us!" Floundering in the deep snow, the machiners are quickly overtaken by the blizzard. Most are unable to see the trail or even the snow machiner directly in front of them. Some are forced to drop their precious cargo sleds to make it back to safety. All in all, one snowmachine and four cargo sleds are left abandoned on the Yukon River, ten miles out of Tanana. Unfortunately, this storm is only the beginning of their troubles.

From my jump seat in the Cessna, I catch fleeting glimpses of the Yukon below as storms rolling over the river yield occasional, breathtaking views. It is an uncomfortable and restless flight, not for myself alone, but for the twenty-three huskies who continue to cower behind me, tight as sardines in a can. After forty minutes, the pitching and yawing Cessna makes a turning descent towards a snowfield situated on a high bluff above the Yukon River. As we glide easily over the snowfield to our landing, there are no buildings or people to welcome our lonely arrival.

"Fear of Flying"
Two of Alana Kingsley's sled dogs huddle together atop
some of the other huskies during the forty minute flight to Ruby

The Cessna taxis to an bouncing stop, and as the engine shuts down, our pilot orders us from the plane. The sun is already settling over the Yukon, which leaves the pilot little time on the ground. With out delay, our gear, all of it, is hastily removed from the plane and piled in disarray on the ice. The dogs are crying to get out of the Cessna as I hasten to gather two snowhooks and a picket line to secure them once they are removed from the plane. I'm wondering how we are supposed to find our way into Ruby with the dogs and gear when suddenly two vintage snowmachines roar out of nowhere. Alana and I are relived to learn they are local villagers, who have come to assist our dog teams into Ruby.

One of them, a soft spoken Athabascan named Billy, instructs me to attach my dog team's gangline to the front of his snowmachine while he hurries to load my dogsled and scattered supplies into a small cargo sled. There is no time to even harness the dogs, and as each of them are freed from their pickets on the Cessna, they leap frantically, one by one, into my arms. It is chaos. But after several heart pounding minutes, Alana and I have hooked up all twenty-three huskies in two teams attached to the snowmachines and are on our way into Ruby. All that is except for poor Bacon, whom I forced to leave behind, temporarily tethered to a solitary sign post on the airstrip. In my haste to connect all the dogs by their collars to the gangline, a small altercation breaks out, leaving Bacon with a minor wound and bleeding at the face. Not wanting to risk further injury to him while the dogs are under stress, I decide to return for him after the rest of the team is secured in Ruby.

Jumping on the back of the snowmachine, Billy calls up my team and we speed away from the airstrip as Bacon's howls of protest fade into the distance. The trip into Ruby goes smoothly and after a short run, the team turns onto a steep, snow covered roadway leading down to the Yukon River hundreds of feet below. At a place high on the hillside, Billy stops our team while I rush forward to set up a proper picket line for the dogs. Just ahead of us are the teams of Don Duncan and Margaret Black who arrived an hour earlier on a separate flight. It is good to see them. By the time my dogs are settled, Billy returns with Bacon who is very happy to see me. After an examination of his face, I am relived to see that his wound is only a minor scrape and cleans up easily.

By the time the dogs have been served warm meals, including a hearty ration of meat, the sun is setting over the Yukon. A chilling wind rising from downriver is blowing over the dogs, but sadly, the straw we had shipped to Ruby for their beds, somehow never arrives. After bundling each of them in their blankets, I drop to my knees and set about chopping foxholes into the snow to help shelter each dog. Under the circumstances, it is the best I can do, and as they snuggle into their little holes, I pack snow around them to help deflect the biting wind. Tonight it is going to get very cold.

Rising from my dogs, I seize the moment to witness the splendor of the wintery vista as the setting sun showers the frozen river and snow covered hillsides in a glow of soft pink. My eyes travel westward down the Yukon River all the way to the horizon, our destination for tomorrow. But by day's end, only six of our eight dog teams have safely arrived in Ruby. That evening, we receive a message informing us that the last two dog teams were unable to make it out of Tanana, and that our snowmachine support, bearing most of the expedition's supplies, is floundering somewhere on the Yukon.

It is unsettling to realize that our once cohesive expedition is now fragmented along a one hundred and twenty mile stretch of the unyielding Yukon River. We are now utterly and completely on our own.

"Ruby Sunset"
Birch, Willow, Bacon, Grits, Tigger, and Chewbacca prepare to settle
in for a long, cold night camped high above the frozen Yukon River

Photo credit: Don Duncan

"The Long Cold Run"
Grits (L) and Willow (R) lead Von's team of eleven huskies under clear blue skies
during the fifty-two mile run on the frozen Yukon River between Ruby and Galena.
Before sunset, Chewbacca was returned to lead position for the final chilling hours of the run.

The Spell of the Yukon

"Most amazing was God's forethought, how wondrous was his plan
- creating the husky dog, the ally and friend of man"

- Charles E. Gillham

March 1st, 2009

At 5:30 am, our team of six mushers awaken in the predawn darkness to prepare for the fifty-two mile run from Ruby to Galena. Stepping outside, we are snapped to attention by the brisk, chilling breeze blowing upriver from the frozen Yukon. Working by headlamp at sub-zero temperatures, I hasten to prepare warm meals for each of my huskies, who for the time, remain curled in their tiny foxholes. Afterwards, I work my way through the picket line, petting each dog and talking to them along the way. I'm doing my best to arouse them with words of encouragement as it is going to be a long, cold run on the Yukon River, and particularly so during the final, chilling night-time hours.

"8:52 am - temperature is 3 degrees. Last night Don Duncan was able to get a call out on a phone for instructions . . . today we are to proceed to Galena on our own without snowmachine support. Erin and Rob, who could not get a flight out yesterday, are flying from Tanana to Galena with their dog teams this afternoon. We have learned that our expedition support team got stuck on the Yukon River outside of Tanana. There was also a medical emergency with one of our team members. The Siglin (cargo) sleds were disconnected and left on the Yukon and the snowmachine teams returned to Tanana. The locals tell us that there is still no travel between Ruby and Tanana at this time. Snow was drifting five feet high on a trail that was clear the previous day and now there is no passage through by anybody. The expedition is in jeopardy at this point."

"It doesn't look like our snowmachine support is going to make it through. We are now one hundred and twenty miles past them at this point. We cannot proceed beyond Galena without their support as they're carrying (most of) the food for our dogs. I'm sure there'll be a rather serious meeting (in Galena) as we assess the expedition as a whole. God Bless our dogs."

"Last night our group of six mushers had a somewhat grim meeting to discuss exactly what we should take on our sleds and how we would arrange for our departure from Ruby. We're going to take only what we need for the fifty-two mile 'march'. We're packing one day's supply of food for ourselves and our dogs, plus snacks . . . we have blankets for the dogs and our cookers. Between the six of us, we have approximately three gallons of HEET for our cookers. We're packing coolers for mixing dog food, our sleeping bags and have our best (arctic) weather gear."

"The dogs spent a very cold night just off the Yukon River in Ruby. The mushers slept on the floor in the Ruby Community Center and I think a lot of us had a fitful night's sleep. But today we have been blessed with good, fair weather and we are hopeful it carries us safely all the way to Galena. We have no weather forecast but Don has a barometer and the (barometric) pressure has been holding steady for the last twelve hours, so we think we can make it in. We are skirting between storms here. We had a bad storm yesterday and there could be another one within twenty four (hours) so we want to make this fifty-two mile run in safe time. The trail is not marked but if today's good weather holds, we should be

Prior to our departure from Ruby, it is agreed that we will "group up" for the night in the off-hand event we should become pinned down by a fast moving storm on the Yukon River. A night spent alone on the river during a serious storm could present a life-threatening hazard. Even as a group, weathering a storm on the Yukon without proper shelter is something we pray we will not have to experience.

Fortunately, both Ruby and our destination, Galena, are designated "drop bag" points on the expedition route. So we are well supplied and there will be ample food to carry along on today's run. After packing our sleds with what we can carry, we donate all that remains of our drop bag supplies to the villagers. At the old community center, I offer an elderly woman and her granddaughter a supply of chemical hand warmers. To another villager, I make the gift of several pounds of meat for his own sled dogs. The gifts are greatly appreciated.

Photo credit: Amy Whisler

"Air Portage Over the Yukon"
A single engine Cessna bearing two dog teams, sleds, and drivers
as photographed from the snowmachine team on the Yukon River

At 10:00 am we send out the first dog teams. By mutual agreement, it is decided to send the girls first, as they are driving the fastest teams. Unfortunately, one of the expedition team members failed to pack dog harness in Tanana, and there is a scramble to find some locally in Ruby. When Emmitt Peters, a resident of Ruby and former Iditarod Champion hears of the situation, he generously lends the "vintage" harnesses worn by his winning dog team back in 1974. The loan is accepted by the driver in need and a potential disaster is narrowly avoided.

Once Don and I have seen the dog teams of Val, Kathy, Ilana, and Margaret safely out of Ruby, we hook up his twelve Samoyeds, one by one, to the gangline attached to his sled. As I kneel at the front of his team, I am struck - almost for the first time - at how petite, yet sturdy, his cheerful assemblage of twelve white "fur balls" really are. I am thinking about how small they seem when measured against the vastness of the Yukon River, of our travels across Alaska, and how this experience rests squarely on the dog's ability - *their desire* - to pull us every mile down the length of this trail. The next thing I know, I'm fighting back a lump in my throat as I realize, once again, what heroic little "guys and gals" these dogs truly are.

Before his departure from Ruby, Don's mood turns solemn as he addresses me at the front of his team. "Enjoy this run Von," he says with a reserved smile. "Make the most of every mile. This *could* be our last day on the trail." There is a distinct emphasis on the word "could". I knew in my heart it was just Don's way of reminding me to "stay in the moment" during today's long run. I was encouraged to make the most of this day, and for a time, not to be concerned with the consequences of our expedition's shortcomings. It would prove to be very sound advice. Likewise, it would echo another of the many life lessons taught to me by my dogs.

"As I was hooking up Duncan's team, we saw Erin and Rob fly over in their plane and gave them a wave, so perhaps they saw us. We're hoping for a safe passage down this steep and treacherous hill onto the river without injury to the dogs. In spite of this hazard, I'm looking forward to the next leg."

"I left Ruby with eleven dogs in harness - Chewbacca and Grits in lead, at 1:00 pm. This morning, Don and I teamed up to get the girls going. By the time Francis, our native coordinator, got around to assisting me through the village with his snowmachine, I had my dogs harnessed and we were off in three or four minutes. After driving my team through Ruby, exactly where the 1925 Serum Run dogs are pictured in a historic photograph, we dropped down onto the Yukon River without any trouble."

Photo credit: Don Duncan

"Shadow on the Yukon"
The silhouetted shadow of musher Don Duncan casts its solitary form
upon the frozen Yukon River during the run from Ruby to Galena

"I was the last team to leave as I was helping everyone else get out. I've got Duncan and his team of Samoyeds in my sights. I'm closing range on him slowly . . . he's about a quarter or third of a mile ahead of me and I'll probably close range on him within a half hour. I'm really hoping this trail hardens up 'cause fifty mile of this (soft trail) is going to kick our butts. That would make it ten hours at best . . . I'm targeting about 11:00 pm - with darkness settling in after 7:00 pm - so that's four hours of darkness on the Yukon. If we don't get any wind I guess that'll be alright. I'll be into my (heavy) mitts by that time. Nevertheless, we want to make the most of it. This could be the last day of our run unless we get some good news from Erin when we arrive in Galena."

"Running Downriver"
Von's team of huskies approaches the team driven by Don Duncan after leaving the village of Ruby
while threading a long, lonely course down the mighty Yukon River in route to Galena

"The snow is very sugary - travel is slow and the dogs are struggling. I did make a leader change because Tigger and Chewy were looking back a bit. This is a section of trail that Willow ran last year (for Iditarod), so I put him in lead with Grits and I've had good success. I put Chewbacca behind the swing dogs with Bacon and he is working very, very hard . . . all of the dogs (are) working very hard now, even Pike and Teak joining in and doing some hard pulling here."

"I'm running approximately in the middle of the Yukon River. There are mountain ranges to my right and there is tundra to my left. It is fairly heavily wooded with black spruce. The Yukon is dotted with islands here and there that look like they're forested with birch. The river is just a barren expanse of ice . . . it looks like Antarctica. It's just ice and not much else to see."

Earlier that day, our snowmachine team rallies for a final attempt to punch a trail from Tanana to Ruby. For the first ten miles, they move somewhat easily over a hard trail, recovering equipment spilled and abandoned on the previous day. Then at 10.3 miles out they encounter waist deep snow. It

Photo credit: Amy Whisler

"Retreat on the Yukon"
Serum Run Expedition team members struggle with a floundered snowmachine on the banks of the Yukon River
March 1, 2009

is hard going with their low speed working machines pulling ten-foot cargo sleds loaded with "600 pounds of dog food, tents, gas, stake out chains, dog kennels, survival gear, and straw bales . . ."

During their struggle to make headway through deep snow, at least one cargo load falls apart. So soft is the trail that after several hours of effort, only fifteen of the one hundred and twenty miles to Ruby is advanced. Later, the team is intercepted by trail breakers, Paul and Kent, who report that "twenty miles out the snow is up to your head with no bottom". Faced with the realization they are battling an impassable trail, our snowmachine team is forced to surrender any hope of gaining more ground. So great is the strain experienced during their retreat, that one team member collapses with chest pains. Finally, at 10:00 pm the defeated team slinks back into Tanana, cold, wet and completely exhausted.

In the meantime, a native showmachiner from Ruby, who set out to break trail in the direction of

Photo credit: Don Duncan

"A Long Way To Nome"
With over four hundred miles still remaining to their final destination, Von Martin and his team of
eleven huskies mush on the Yukon River en route to Galena, approximately midway to Nome

Tanana, is reported missing on the Yukon River. Thirty-six hours later, 'Search and Rescue' finds him
holed up in a trapper cabin, unable to continue. That evening, the expedition's lead veterinarian, Jerry
Vanek, summarizes the support teams declining moral as they consider their situation in Tanana. "Two
broken snowmachines, dwindling food, gas, money, and one mild heart attack later, we're realizing we
have to pull the plug. Then an esteemed village elder walks up and tells us not to go west, she senses a
very bad omen about us continuing on. We get the message."

Earlier that day, as the snowmachine team struggled to break trail nearly one hundred and fifty
miles upriver, our dog teams continue to out-distance them. Unaware of their hardship, we thread a
course toward Galena along the mile wide Yukon River. As the sun drops toward the horizon, the temperature, likewise, spirals steadily downward until it registers minus double digits. At these temperatures, one of the challenges faced by mushers is maintaining proper hydration. Containers of Gatorade,
and other high impact drinks freeze quickly, even when stowed in the sled bag. These are the first to be
consumed. Next are three bottles of high energy drinks that I have stuffed inside my snowsuit to keep
from freezing solid during the run. Once these are exhausted, I have only the hydration supplied by my
Camelback device, an insulated thermos worn under my snowsuit. Water from the Camelback is delivered by means of a tube running under my arm to a small valve tucked inside my collar just out of the
wind. In spite of these precautions, temperatures drop so low that the delivery tube inside my snowsuit
begins to freeze, making it increasingly difficult to draw water. After several hours of mind numbing
cold, together with the slowly emerging effects of dehydration, my audio log entry hints at the early
onset of hypothermia as I briefly struggle to recall my destination while driving my dog team downriver.

"The is the Serum Run update for . . . I have to remember where I'm at . . . I'm on my way to Galena from . . . ahh . . . from Ruby. The time is 6:17 pm. The sun is two degrees above the horizon and is setting like a big orange orb directly over the Yukon River spreading out before us. Intermittently rising from the river, are shards of ice anywhere from several inches to a couple feet tall that are backlit from the sun and shining like pieces of Chihuly glass art above the frozen Yukon River. It's just beautiful."

"We have been running for five hours and nineteen minutes nonstop, except for a five minute snack break. Duncan (is) behind me . . ohh . . . half a mile at the most. Winds are calm and skies are absolutely, perfectly clear. The dogs are moving along nicely but the trail continues to vary between a 4 and 5 mph slog through sugary snow with a few (hard) patches that allows the team to pick up to about seven miles an hour at best. So it's slow, slow progress. The scenery doesn't change much. You've got a river bank on the right and a river bank on the left. Presently, I'm only yards from the left bank that has brush growing on it. The right bank, which is at least half a mile away, is forested and hilly. The

Photo credit: Don Duncan

"A Speck on the Landscape"
The dog team of Von Martin is dwarfed in the distance against the scale of the Yukon River
as photographed from the team of Samoyeds driven by musher Don Duncan

sun is directly in front of us, setting down over the Yukon River. I have no idea of how far we've traveled. By my estimate at 5 mph that puts us about twenty-five miles into our run of fifty-two miles, and darkness will be settling over us within the hour."

Just before the sun meets the horizon, I stop my team and hook down. Besides the fact it is already becoming very cold, I want to take advantage of the remaining minutes of daylight to feed frozen meat snacks to all my huskies, inspect their feet, change booties as needed, and make final adjustments to the tuglines. While caring for my dogs, Don Duncan pulls up behind me with his team of Samoyeds and also hooks down. Directly in front of us, the sun is about to converge with the horizon. It is a magnifi-

Photo credit: Don Duncan

"Sunset at 22 Degrees Below Zero"
Von Martin looks back from his dogsled over the team of Samoyeds driven by musher
Don Duncan as the sun dips below the horizon over the frozen Yukon River

cent and breathtaking scene. As I stand and relish the last rays of the sun, Don calls out the temperature from the back of his sled. "Minus twenty-two degrees!" My mind reels with his announcement. If the temperature has already plunged to twenty-two degrees below zero *before* sunset, then just how cold, I wonder, is it going to get over the next several hours?

Neither Don or I can be absolutely sure how many miles we have already traveled. Likewise, there is no way to be sure how many hours of running lie ahead of us before our arrival into Galena. Two years ago, along this same stretch of trail, a Serum Run dog team "shut down", that is, refused to move another mile. Fortunately, they were assisted by the expedition's snowmachine support team. However for Don and I, there would be no hope of rescue if either of our dog teams decide to shut down. We can only trust that our dogs are physically, and *mentally* prepared to continue non-stop all the way to Galena, no matter how many hours distant.

Working hastily with ungloved hands, I examine each dog on the team while changing several of their booties. At minus twenty-two, exposed hands can quickly "stove up" and before long, I'm forced to plunge my hands back into my heavy mitts. To help combat the extreme cold, I deposit fresh chemical hand warmers into each of them before shuffling through deep snow at the edge of the trail to the front of my dog team. Icicles are already forming at their muzzles, and their coats have begun to assume a layer of ice produced by their exhaled breath which drifts over the lengths of their backs while underway.

Before departing for the coldest, most challenging stretch of the run, I return Chewbacca to his rightful position as lead dog with Grits at the front of the team. Even as the twilight is reflected in their eyes I can see they are ready to resume their run. I'm remembering that "Chewy" has never let me down when the going gets tough. Somehow I know with this capable, nearly eleven year old leader at the front of my team, everything is going to be alright. With a wave to Don, I remount my sled runners, release each snowhook from the ice, and pull away, quite literary, into the sunset.

In a minute or two the sun dips below the horizon. Shortly, twilight gives way to darkness and without trail markers to direct the way, Chewy and Grits continue to pick out a westward course to Galena. With only the sliver of a crescent moon and the stars to illuminate the way, the dogs continue downriver at an even trot mile after mile. Finally, after hours of running in darkness, a faint glow appears on the horizon. At first I am encouraged that it is the far off light of Galena coming into view. Yet after a time, the light eventually fades, and once again we are threading our way downriver without a visible destination.

From time to time, I switch on my headlamp to check the condition and progress of the dogs. Drifting past the fur ruff of my hooded parka are millions of tiny, sparkling crystals. So cold and dry is the air, that each exhaled breath from my huskies immediately condenses into a cloud of icy fog drifting back over the team. As it has been at least two hours since our last stop and a check for the condition of the dog's booties, I call the team to a halt and hook down the sled. Working by the light of my headlamp, I begin making my way to the front of the team. Halfway there I realize something about the them doesn't seem right. In fact, I can't recognize a single dog on my team. At first I think I must be hallucinating, that somehow I am no longer driving my own dogs. Arriving at the front of the team, I cast the light of my headlamp down the length of the dogs to the sled. I am driving a team of pure white huskies. Each and every one of them is completely white from their tips of their muzzles to the ends of their tails.

Suddenly, as if signaled by an unseen hand, the entire team of dogs simultaneously shake their coats, resulting in an explosive cloud of crystals and ice. Almost miraculously, familiar faces emerge through the dissipating cloud of white "fairy dust". First I recognize Chewbacca, then Grits. In a moment the cheerful faces of little Tigger and Cherry come into view. Then the familiar coats of Willow, Birch, Bacon, Pike, Teek, Patrick, and Boomer reappear! I am driving my own dogs again. Nearly all of them are wagging their tails, even though it has been almost ten hours since our departure from Ruby. Yet there is still no visible light from Galena on the horizon. Since sunset, the temperature has continued to plunge and I can only guess that by now it must be greater than *thirty* below. I have no idea how long I can expect my dogs to keep running as I have never asked them to run continuously for more than eleven hours. I think back to the group dinner in Willow before the expedition when I was told that my dogs are capable of doing much more than I think they can. Tonight I was going to find out. After stopping to pet each dog on the way back to my sled, I remount the runners and pull the

Photo credit: Don Duncan

"No Jacket Required"

Naturally adapted for polar travel, Don Duncan's heavy coated Samoyeds, such as Quilly seen here during the night-time run to Galena, can easily withstand freezing temperatures greater than 50 degrees below zero

snowhooks. Switching off my headlamp, I call out to Chewbacca. In seconds we are gliding along in darkness to the place where the stars meet the horizon. Still, I am encouraged with the thought that we are not alone. Somewhere out in the darkness, following at an unseen distance, are Don Duncan and his team of gallant Samoyeds.

Within the hour, an odd feature drifts past my dog sled only inches away. Even in the night I can see it is something slender and wiry sticking up from the trail. Whirling my head around, I flick on my head lamp. Caught in the pure white glow of the halogen beam are the familiar yellow and orange reflectors fastened to the tip of a Serum Run trail marker. Someone has set trails markers leading into Galena!

Through Wolfie's ice encrusted wool scarf wrapped around my face, I cry out to the dogs, "It's a Serum Run marker guys. We're on the trail into Galena!" Their response to my encouragement is nearly instantaneous as they bend deeper into their harnesses and increase speed. But the show is just for me. By following the "scent trail" set down by dog teams ahead of us, my huskies know they are tracking a precise course. Unfortunately, neither the dogs nor I know just *how* much further we must be expected to travel.

Shortly, a faint light appears in the distance near the shoreline of the river. In time, the light grows into a small string of lights that seem to beckon us on. About every two hundred yards another Serum Run trail marker makes an appearance as the dogs, now moving at a quick trot, thread a course toward the faint lights. However, after a time the trail carries us beyond the lights. One by one, they drift by on our right before dimming faintly behind us. "Could we have missed a cutoff into Galena in the darkness," I wonder? Meanwhile, the trail markers continue to make their steady appearance, beckoning us further downriver, and ever further from the lure of the lights, now disappeared completely from view.

Hoping for a clue, I flick on my headlamp. It reveals only an icy trail slipping further into the gaping Yukon River, seized in a silent, frozen drift. Suddenly, for the first time Chewy stops. He looks back at me, and in his eyes I see the doubt that, by now, he must also be sensing in me. This was no time for the team to shut down. Perhaps that *was* Galena we just passed. Perhaps it was not. Somewhere beyond the shoreline, the faint din of a dog team can be heard. But whose dogs? And from where? It is a defining moment. We had been running for eleven hours and I cannot expect the dogs to continue much longer. I could not jeopardize their trust that I would deliver them to safe haven and *soon.*

I hooked down the sled and walked to the front of the team. Kneeling before Chewy and Grits I address them in a calm, steady voice, "OK guys, here's the deal. We'll run for fifteen more minutes. If the trail doesn't take us off the river into Galena by that time, we'll turn around and take the first cut-off into whatever place we just passed, alright?" I gently stroked Chewy's head with a heavy mitt before casting my headlamp down the line of eleven huskies who are nearing the end of their endurance. Ice dangles in long needle-like shards from their lips and their coats have mostly reassumed their ghostly, white appearance.

As I return to the sled, the dogs turn, one by one, to study me as I pass by. Given the very cold temperatures and the incredible effort they have made since leaving Ruby, I'm reasonably sure they can't give me more than another thirty minutes. And I won't ask them to. Remounting the sled's runners one last time, I pull the snowhooks and call out to my "canine buddy" at the front of the team. "Alright Chewy, let's go boy." He responds without hesitation, bending into his harness in a way that encourages every dog to follow suit. The gallant effort of each dog is pulling at my heartstrings as I marvel not only at their ability, but for their unshakeable loyalty to me as well. In return, I realize they are trusting me to deliver them to a place of rest.

For several agonizing minutes, the dogs continue to follow the trail markers set every one hundred yards or so. In a moment of doubt, I begin to worry that perhaps these markers have been placed here to help lead us out of Galena during the next day's run - that perhaps we have already passed an unseen cutoff into the village. It is a fearful thought. The cold is absolutely numbing, particularly so after nearly eleven hours on the runners. Yet in spite of these hardships, I can think only about the dogs and the difficulties that will be presented if I am forced to turn them around in complete darkness without slipping off the trail.

Suddenly, from out of the blackness, appears a steady string of trail markers tightly grouped just a few feet apart. Following their course, Chewy and Grits navigate a wide sweeping turn off the river and up a long embankment. We are off the Yukon! What follows next is tricky as we enter a maze of snow covered roadways and intersections, guided by the reflectors of Serum Run trail markers. Along the way we pass buildings and chain link fencing, as the dogs move at a quick trot, encouraged with the imminent promise of a well deserved rest and meal. Rounding a wide turn, we suddenly come upon a resting team, and in a moment I recognize them as Margaret's beautiful Siberian Huskies. At the same time, I am greeted by a familiar voice that directs us to our "parking spot". It is the welcome voice of Erin McLarnon, our expedition team leader. The dogs have done it. They never quit.

It is shortly before midnight, and so cold are my hands, that I am unable to remove the brass snaps from the dog's tuglines. Erin jumps in to assist me while making the *heavenly* gift of a pair of warm gloves, heated with fresh chemical hand warmers. As I set about making straw beds for each dog and to prepare their warm meals, Don Duncan pulls into view with his gorgeous team of Samoyeds. I am so happy to see his team I could almost burst. We are all safely in Galena. Above the din of barking huskies and Samoyeds, Don's voice calls out to me, "Minus 38 degrees!" It has been a long cold run. Yet it is not truly over until I have offered hugs to my huskies, every single one of them.

"All Dressed Up and Nowhere to Go"
The dogs sit dressed in their blankets at Galena while anxiously awaiting their next run to Nulato.
Sadly, the expedition was shut down minutes later when the snowmachine support team announced it was
unable to rendezvous with the dog teams. Visible L to R in foreground are Boomer, Patrick, Pike, and Teek

Bidding the Dream Farewell

"You don't always make it the first time, but you just keep trying. It's all an adventure"

- Col. Norman D. Vaughan

March 2nd, 2009 - Serum Run Log

"The time is 7:20 pm - the location is Galena, Alaska. The temperature is 12 degrees below zero. Skies are mostly cloudy and there is another storm approaching."

"My team arrived in Galena just before midnight. It was a non-stop eleven hour run. The temperature was 38 degrees below zero but they looked wonderful. I could not jacket them as their jackets were frozen solid and could not be opened due to the cold temperatures from Ruby and the damp weather we had experienced since Tanana. Today I was able to thaw them indoors and this evening they are enjoying dry jackets."

"At exactly 10:16 am this morning, we received a phone call from Tanana to report that a vote by the snowmachine support team had determined that they were going to turn back and our expedition was over. It was a huge disappointment, especially when our dogs arrived looking so good last night."

"After getting the news, I went out to my dog team and talked with each of them. I began with Chewbacca. I told him what a magnificent job he did and how very proud I am of him. I told each of them that they had exceeded my greatest expectations. I didn't know my dogs could march for eleven or twelve hours without stops, except for five minute snack breaks, or to change a bootie, or look after an ankle, adjust a harness, or to just rub their ears and offer them a kind word. They are

Photo credit: Don Duncan

"Eleven Little Heroes"
Chewbacca (foreground) and Von's team of huskies await
the return of their "Master" to the dog lot in Galena where
early morning temperatures dropped to minus 42 degrees

amazing. They are perfect little creatures. I shed my tears privately with my dogs. If I have a regret, it's only that they didn't have the opportunity to fulfill what I had hoped was their legacy."

After spending time with each dog on the team, there remained one final dog to honor. Reaching into the sled's cargo bag, I reverently remove the little round tin container bearing Wolfie's ashes.

Slightly dented but still intact after many miles on the trail, its condition somehow reflects the wear and tear of our long journey together.

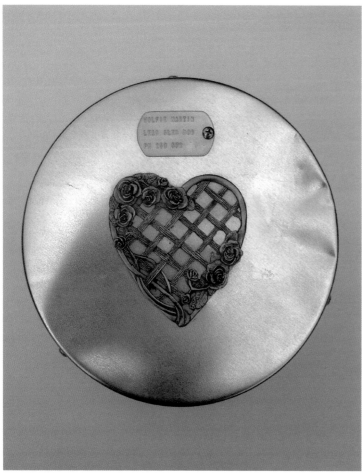

"A Promise Remembered"
Wolfie's tin of ashes accompanied Von's sled dog team
every mile of the 2009 Serum Run '25 expedition

For a time, I study her tin in silence while kneeling in the snow near the dogs. Then in soft words, I privately honor her memory with a song I had reserved for the end of our journey together. Entitled "The Promise" by songwriter, Ted Martin, it is a richly nostalgic song that begins;

> *"Here we are at the end of the road,*
> *Lookin' back I wouldn't change a thing at all"*

Afterwards, I can't help thinking back to that day in 2005 when I let Wolfie go, and of my promise to include her on a trip to Nome by dog team.

"Well girl, we didn't get to Nome," I apologized. "But I guess we came just about as far as we were meant to go." As I rise to my feet, I realize how small and fragile her little box of ashes feels in my hands. Weighing less than four pounds, it is only a fraction of the nearly eighty pounds she once weighed in life. During the expedition, I even had thoughts about leaving a little of her on the shores of Nome, so that a part of her would always be there at the end of the trail.

Even after death, there is a part of these noble and heroic dogs that never leaves you. Their powerful spirit remains with you wherever you are on the trail, until that time when you finally meet again. For the next several minutes I lingered there alone with the dogs - thinking of all that had happened - and what would never be. With a gentle pat of Wolfie's little tin I tell her, "Thanks just the same 'ole girl. Thanks for helping to show the way here."

Serum Run Log (continued)

"These dogs have not only taught me what they are capable of but of what they are willing to do for you. The march last night was very cold - the snow was deep. It was only fifty-two miles but it was very slow and very, very hard work for them. Hour after hour I marveled at their steady trot down that trail. It is amazing, it is wonderful, and it's miraculous what they can do. I don't know how those little bodies can move so long and work so hard."

"All the dogs are in remarkably good condition. I want it on record that when I came out to the dog lot this morning, that every single one of them leaped to attention and wagged their tails. And had I

"Boomer's Pillow"
Boomer, one of two powerful wheel dogs on Von's Serum Run team, enjoys a soft bed of straw and
"pillow" of snow while basking in the afternoon sun as temperatures warmed to a balmy 10 degrees
Galena, Alaska

*harnessed them, and said, 'We're going to Nulato', they would have taken me there - right now. They
are the fittest I've ever seen them. They have grown stronger everyday. I had no idea they could do
this. We didn't get to Nome but they showed me what they can do. Those dogs and this expedition have
taught me a lot about myself. It is the hardest thing I have ever done. I am so grateful to my wife, to my
friends, and to my family for helping to make this experience possible."*

*"So here we are one hundred and seventy-six miles downriver from our support team. Our dogs are
fit, our drop bags are here, our sleds are equipped and we could move on but we don't have the support team. They move three days worth of food at a time for us. But even if we could get to Nulato,
there's talk that the Kaltag Portage is impassable all the way out to the coast. And there's another
storm due tonight and four more behind that we're told. Alaskans don't remember a winter like this
since the very early 80's. Very cold and lots of snow."*

"Evacuation Flight"
A privately chartered DC-6 awaits on the icy airstrip at Galena between snowstorms as mushers and
cargo attendants hurry to evacuate over eighty huskies and the expedition's dogsleds to Anchorage, Alaska
March 4th, 2009

"There is still a lot of hard work ahead as we try and figure out how to get dog (shipment) boxes to Galena. It's a small village, not as small as Ruby or Old Minto, but it sits here on the Yukon. We need to fly (the dogs) to Anchorage. Although there is no passenger service to Anchorage from here, I can get a little plane to Fairbanks and then take an Alaska Air flight to Anchorage where I'll rejoin my dogs. My understanding is that once the snowmachine team makes its way back to Nenana, that everything from the expedition (carried) on the Siglin cargo sleds will be put on a train or a truck to Anchorage. I would be pleased as punch to recover all of it once I'm back there with my dog truck. Then up to Fairbanks to recover Jack. And then the long drive home."

March 3rd, 2009 - Serum Run Log

"The time is 4:00 pm from Galena, Alaska. Temperature is 10 degrees, skies are very clear and no wind. The dogs are doing well. The sun is out and they're enjoying the sunny afternoon. They still have their jackets on. I've got kibble to last at least five days and twenty pounds of meat so we're not down on our luck for dog food yet. But we still cannot get the dogs out of Galena. There is no dog box ship-

ment available out of Nome. The plane is in Anchorage where they keep waiting for a window that would allow them to fly into Nome to pick up the boxes and get them back to Galena. With every passing hour they still can't do it because there are blizzards on the coast. So we have no way out of the village. I should name this chapter, 'My Galena Vacation'.

"In the meantime, the school has continued to host us with warm dry rooms and the cooking school is providing us with meals. I have very limited phone access and no internet access. I haven't seen a toothbrush in over a week and have been in the same clothes since I left Washington the first of February. I did have an undergarment wash in Manley. But if I'm stuck here another day, I'm going to hook up my dogs and go for a run on the Yukon."

"I'm hearing we made the 10:00 pm news across Alaska. We also made the front page of the Alaska

"No More Trail "
Still fully packed with gear and supplies, two of the Serum Run '25 Expedition dogsleds are carried
by forklift to a chartered cargo plane for return shipment to Anchorage, Alaska. Due to travel restrictions,
the mushers were not allowed to accompany their huskies on the early morning evacuation flight out of Galena

"Tie a Yellow Ribbon"
Air freight boxes, each carrying ten expedition huskies, are fork lifted to an awaiting cargo plane. Each door is marked with a colored ribbon identifying the owner of the team. Boxes bearing Von's dogs are marked with yellow ribbons

Daily News with 'Serum Run Shut Down Due to Weather'. I talked to Billy who is a native of Ruby and asked, 'How often have you seen weather like this in Alaska?' He said he remembered one time in the early '80's and before that when he was only a youngster. So these are epic storms. The talk is now turning to what will happen for Iditarod because the Kaltag Portage is still not open. There are several days of blizzard force winds slated for the coast and continued cold temperatures. There is still no travel on the Yukon between Ruby and Tanana."

March 4th, 2009 - Serum Run Log

"The time is 4:07 am from Galena, Alaska. Temperature is approximately 20 below. At 2:30 am, a four engine, vintage model DC-6 bearing all our huskies numbering nearly eighty, and seven dogsleds departed the airstrip at Galena for Anchorage. Around midnight, we shuttled our dogs in little open boxes towed by a snowmobile - each musher riding with their dogs to keep them calm - from the dog lot to the airstrip which is covered in snow and ice. There we transferred our dogs from the shuttle boxes

into shipping boxes filled with fresh straw to make them comfortable. We put them inside their little apartments and bolted the doors closed. Afterwards a forklift came by. First they loaded our sleds, then they loaded our 'babies' onto the plane."

"When they lit up those four big engines, we just stood there in the darkness with the snow falling all around. Then we watched in silence as the airplane roared to the end of the airstrip, rose slowly upwards, and disappeared into the night. It was a very sobering moment. And I wasn't alone in my tears. So now they are headed to Anchorage. And Chewy, I love you. I'm so sorry I won't see your face in Nome. You are all such good dogs."

On the afternoon of March 5th, 2009, we are finally able to secure passage on a small commuter flight out of Galena to Fairbanks. Still attired in our expedition outfits and packing only our sleeping bags, we then board a connecting flight to Anchorage. Shortly after midnight on March 6th, I arrive at the home of my Alaska host family where I celebrate a bittersweet reunion with my dogs who awaken to welcome my arrival. Even little Sol-leks is there to greet me with fond kisses and that night he enjoys the solitary privilege of sharing my bed in the house.

As we drift off to sleep, I talk to him of our adventures on the trail and how much I missed him in the team. It is a moment of great comfort and I am aglow with the thought that in another day or two I will be picking up Blackjack as we swing through Fairbanks on our long drive home to Washington.

"An Early End to the Expedition"
More than 80 huskies are carefully loaded on board a chartered DC-6 for shipment back to Anchorage, Alaska.
A brief "weather window" between blizzards required a hasty departure after midnight before the next storm arrived
Galena, Alaska

"No Serum for Nome"
An undelivered vial of "Serum" from the 2009 Serum Run '25 Expedition bears
the words of Col. Norman Vaughan's iconic challenge to "Dream Big & Dare to Fail"

Life Lessons Learned

"When I look into my dog's eyes,
I can see God's love looking back at me"

- Dee Dee Jonrowe

This is a story about overcoming adversity in an extreme situation, of counting your blessings, and recognizing your achievements even if a "goal" wasn't achieved. More particularly, it is a tribute to my "family" of sled dogs who made it possible for us to accept Col. Norman Vaughan's legendary challenge to "Dream Big and Dare to Fail".

When making my application to the 2009 Serum Run '25 Expedition, I was asked for my reason to participate. Looking back at our experience on the trail, I can appreciate that my greatest reason for participating was fully realized when I answered with,

"Running in the footsteps of those hearty dogs of 1925, together with their drivers,
will bring an appreciation of their accomplishment that can be known in no other way".

In an age when the most advanced communication technology consisted only of primitive telegraph and telephone service, before the development of advanced dogsled and harness designs, electronic navigation devices, or high tech arctic clothing, those original twenty mushers and their amazing dogs somehow prevailed. Armed only with their courage and unshakeable determination, they struggled through one of the worst Alaskan winters on record to successfully relay 300,000 units of anti-toxin to Diphtheria stricken Nome. To say that I have been humbled by their miraculous achievement would be an understatement. After setting out to honor their legacy in 2009, those heroic men and their dogs will forever reign in my heart as the unparalleled champions of the trail.

March 4th, 2009 - Serum Run Log

"Was the 2009 Serum Run a success or a failure? I really believe it's a matter of your perspective. Did the 'Serum' get delivered to Nome? No. But if you look at a journey as a process and not as an objective, I think it was a great success. When I consider the amazing successes that occurred on this trip, of what I learned and of the challenges met, it has been one of the most successful endeavors of my life. Throughout this experience, I learned much about dog care, traveling in extreme weather, and living in an arctic environment. Did I know that my dogs could run for eleven hours in snow over their knees and up to their bellies at 38 below? Did I know that I could endure those kinds of temperatures day after day? I don't think I'll ever be quite the same after this. I have been changed by this experience and in a very good way. I was told the (expedition) will change you. This has been a very good chapter in my life and a lot of good has come out of it. It has been life at its best - with love - heartbreak - and triumph."

"There are so many things that happened on this expedition that caught me by surprise. Looking back, it was often the inverse experience of everything I expected to happen. I learned how to take success out of failure. I also gained a greater appreciation for what my dogs can do. Finally, I learned a lot from other people. I was blessed to receive countless gestures of kindness by so many people. It was a very good experience."

"I've had some amazing opportunities on this journey. Meeting the villagers, talking with the children, mentoring students and encouraging them. Through all of this I hope that I have done God's work in a way that is pleasing to him. I have thoroughly enjoyed this experience and I would do it everyday for the rest of my life if I could. It has been so fulfilling. It is also the hardest thing I have ever done. I don't know if I'll ever see Nome. But I was a part this expedition to honor those original mushers and their dogs. And we gave it our best effort."

"Almost from the beginning, the entire expedition seemed to have this 'jinx' in it. But working day by day, sometimes hour by hour to make last minute changes and amendments, we did our best in a loosing battle against adversity. In doing so, I

Photo credit: Don Duncan

"Going Home"
Von Martin (L) and mushers of the 2009 Serum Run '25 expedition walk to an airstrip for their flight out of Galena

would like to remember this expedition as a big success in terms of how well our team held up. From a missing snowmachiner on the first day of the expedition to a never imagined experience with the dog teams crammed into a small airplane, we made our very best effort to reevaluate circumstances when things seemed to go wrong. By considering our options in a 'talking circle' and putting issues to vote, we found solutions and made decisions quickly. In the process, I have learned much about group dynamics, assessing emergency situations, and working as a team under extreme circumstances. It has been a great experience. I can't think of any workplace that can compare to the incredible mental, physical, and emotional demands that an arctic expedition can place upon you. And out of it comes knowledge and a good feeling about holding up and persevering."

In consideration of how the 2009 Serum Run expedition will be remembered, I recall my comment to fellow musher, Don Duncan, as we prepared our dogs for "air portage" out of Tanana. "Someday," I told Don, "Serum Run mushers will look back on this expedition and say, 'Remember back in '09, when we had to fly all those huskies from Tanana to Ruby on a little Cessna?'" It is interesting to note that historically, most expeditions have resulted in some measure of failure due to the countless risks inherent to them. Further, there is a kind of irony when considering that some of the best remembered polar expeditions were not those that succeeded, but rather those that did not. The details of Scott's failed quest for the South Pole, of Mawson's tragic Antarctic expedition in 1913, and the "grand-daddy" of them all, Shackleton's Endurance Expedition, are more familiar than Amundsen's winning race to the South Pole. Even Col. Norman Vaughan's first attempt to summit the Antarctic mountain bearing his name, resulted in the catastrophic crash of a large airplane, human injury, and the loss of several dogs.

Perhaps God, in His infinite wisdom, had only intended for our team to journey as far as Galena. Looking back, I think there may have been many good reason for this. Considering the poor trail conditions and seemingly endless onslaught of blizzards that besieged the Alaskan coast and interior, our dog teams may have been spared some unknown catastrophe. During the Iditarod Race that immediately followed the Serum Run Expedition, a few mushers experienced a life-threatening brush with an arctic storm that claimed the lives of a least two huskies.

We did not set out on the 2009 Serum Run '25 Expedition to make a case or to prove any particular point. Our intentions, as stated in the expedition's mission statement, was simply to honor those original twenty men and their dogs while delivering messages of health education to rural Alaskan villages. Above all, the safety of our team, and particularly, our dogs was first and foremost. Given the unprecedented trail conditions, to have asked them to continue to Nome from Galena could have risked placing them in peril, or at the very least, to have put them through a miserable experience. In all fairness to our huskies, we could not allow them to do this. We weren't crossing Alaska to set any records or to demonstrate that we were, in any way, more capable than those original dog teams in 1925. Rather, it goes back to the trust these dogs have placed in us to make the best decisions for them, as reflected in the ultimate musher's motto, "It's all about the dogs".

"Real Heroes"
Leonard Seppala and his lead dog Togo, were among the original twenty dog teams in the 1925 relay

Of all the lessons learned during this expedition, the greatest were the unique "life lessons" taught to me by my own dogs. Unlike their human counterparts, the dogs are truly able to "live in the moment", each and every hour of their lives. You see, those dogs never knew they were going to a place called Nome. Rather, with every new dawn, they arose from their beds, shook their coats, and joyfully looked forward to another day. They just couldn't wait to experience the next mile of the journey, to see what awaited around the next turn, and in doing so, thoroughly enjoyed the promise of each new day.

From those twelve dogs I learned that the expedition was about more than leaving Nenana and arriving in Nome. It was about experiencing life every mile, every hour, every *minute* along the way. By extending this lesson to the rest of my life, I realized how those dogs taught me a greater appreciation for living each day between birth and death. They demonstrated that every step of our journey through this life, is not about what we take from it, but rather the pure joy we can experience each day, the gifts we give, and the legacy we leave behind. And of all the gifts these dogs are so utterly capable of teaching, the greatest is love. *Unconditional love.*

I have been often asked if I would ever consider returning to Alaska for another try at the Serum Run '25 expedition. Would I be willing to go through the agonizing months of planning all over again? To return to the hardship of running a dog team across Alaska and experience the freezing cold? Make yet another financial commitment? *In a New York Minute!*

It's like Col. Norman Vaughan used to say. "You don't always make it the first time. You go back and try again. It's all an adventure".

"Welcome Home"
Blackjack receives a warm welcome home by Von's wife, Judith, while Sol-leks looks on.
After the removal of his leg cast, "Jack" made a complete recovery and was returned to active service.

About the Author

Von Martin, an emerging author of books and stories about sled dogs, was born at Camp Pendleton Marine Base in Oceanside, California. He is a member of the Pacific Northwest Writers Association and is a graduate of the University of Hawaii where he was also an instructor in Anthropology. Von's professional careers have also included work as a skilled carpenter, musician, singer, writer, and reporter.

Von is the Vice-President of the Northwest Sled Dog Association and has logged thousands of miles with his own dog team throughout five western states, British Columbia, and Alaska. He is employed as a construction news reporter and works from his rural log cabin home in southwest Washington where he also enjoys caring for his 17 sled dogs. Von is married to Judy, a native of Washington state.

In 2009 Von Martin participated in the Col. Norman Vaughan Serum Run '25 Expedition - an 800 mile midwinter journey by dog team across the frontier of Alaska.

His next book, "A DOG CALLED SHAKESPEARE - Fallen Canine Hero of Shackleton's 1914 Antarctic Expedition", will be his first in a series of books chronicling the legacy of the remarkable dogs employed during the early polar expeditions.

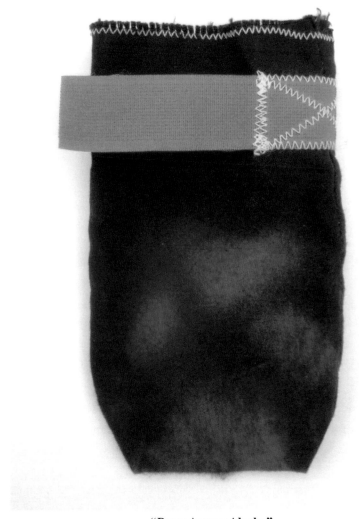

"Paws Across Alaska"
A bootie from Von's sled dog team bearing the indelible footprint of one of
his huskies, paints a poignant portrait of the dog's remarkable journey

Made in the USA
Charleston, SC
08 December 2009